JULY SKY MEDIA, LLC

National Park Guide for Dogs

A handy guide to where you can go in theU.S. National Parks – 2025-2026 Edition

To Koji (lil' Kojaroony)
The sweetest boy who visited 14 US and Canadian National Parks
with me during our travels together.

To Remi (Remi the Road Dog)
My rescue who is the most at peace when we are traveling down the
road and is just starting her National Park adventures.

(Cover photo of Remi as we entered Wind Cave National Park.)

Contents

1

Introduction

Visiting National Parks is not always just a vacation destination. Whether you typically travel with your pets, stop at National Parks as side trips while moving or traveling to other destinations, or visit National Parks as part of a mobile lifestyle, you may have your dog(s) and other pets with you when you visit. Each park has specific rules and access for pets, and it is best to know that before heading into the park to ensure a safe and enjoyable experience for you and your pets. This book focuses on dogs, but most of the regulations are for all domestic pets.

Each National Park is unique, and the amount of access to domestic pets in each park differs. This book is a handy guide to quickly and easily look up the pet information for the parks you are interested in visiting. The parks are listed alphabetically in each section and divided into categories from the most accessible to no access. This guide is the most current information available at the time of writing and publishing. You can find the link to the pet-specific National Park page in each section for the most up-to-date information. You can also access the most current information on most National Park websites by clicking "Plan Your Visit" on the menu bar. A drop-down menu will appear with "Basic Information," from that drop-down, you can find the "Pets" link on most park websites. Park Visitor Centers and Park Rangers can also provide more specific information regarding pet access and programs. Many park websites also provide information and links for nearby pet-friendly areas outside the park.

Due to the limited access for pets in most parks and specific safety concerns and weather concerns at certain times of the year, it is best to know before you go so that you can make alternative arrangements before visiting the park if necessary.

Most of all, this book is meant to help you quickly and easily determine what activities you can enjoy with your dog companions while visiting the U.S. National Parks, especially when you are unable to access the website due to a lack of internet or cell service.

2

"For the Enjoyment and Benefit of the People"

On March 1st, 1872, President Ulysses S. Grant signed The Act of Dedication, which created Yellowstone National Park, the world's first national park. The park status protected the land, unique hydrothermal features, and wildlife. It was Ferdinand V. Hayden whose expedition, the Hayden Geological Survey of 1871, led to the protection of the land. Hayden believed in protecting the land "for the benefit and enjoyment of the people" and foresaw the destruction of the land and wildlife if not protected. This sentiment was included in the legislation that created Yellowstone National Park and is engraved on the Roosevelt Arch, which leads to the North entrance of Yellowstone National Park. Hayden Valley is a popular area to see the wildlife of Yellowstone.

Since 1872, the United States has created 63 National Parks as of 2024. While the national parks primarily protect natural areas or sites of ancient cultural significance, they have also begun to include national historic areas, such as Gateway Arch National Park. The National Park System, which encompasses the current 63 National Parks, also includes over 400 protected areas, including historic parks, national monuments, national lakeshores, national seashores, and other significant natural or historical areas within the United States. Some of these protected areas have become National Parks, and more will likely be added in the future. Visit https://www.nps.gov/findapark to discover all of the areas that are currently part of the national park system.

National Parks have been popular destinations to see beautiful landscapes, unique geological features, hydrothermal features, cave systems, and protected wildlife. They have also been popular destinations for outdoor recreational activities such as hiking, backcountry camping, boating, and rock climbing. Each park is unique in its history and offerings. Because of this, the accessibility to pets is also unique to each park.

It is essential to know and follow the pet policies for each park, not only for the safety of you and your pet but for the safety of the wildlife and the integrity of the park so that the park can continue to be enjoyed by you and generations to come.

In the next chapter, we will explore the basics of pets in the National Parks, from the pet policies that apply to all National Parks to basic pet and trail etiquette.

3

Pets in the Parks: The Basics

Pets are welcome in most National Parks, but many have restricted areas where pets are allowed to visit.

These are the basic restrictions that apply to all National Parks:

- Pets must be on a leash at all times or otherwise contained (crate, vehicle, camper, etc.) The leash may be no longer than 6 feet (1.8m) in length.
- Pets are allowed in parking areas, main roads, picnic areas, and drive-in campgrounds (unless otherwise restricted by the individual park).
- Pets are not allowed in park buildings, including Visitor Centers.
- Pets are not allowed on trails or in the backcountry unless specified by individual parks.
- Pets carried in arms, pet carriers, strollers, backpacks, etc., must follow the same guidelines and restrictions as leashed pets.

- Pets may not be left unattended while tethered outside to any object. (They may attract predatory animals, among other concerns.)
- Pet food and water may not be left unattended outdoors or in a manner that will attract wildlife.
- Pet waste must always be collected, bagged, and placed in a trash bin or dumpster.
- Pets are not allowed to make excessive noise that disturbs wildlife or other visitors.

Learning the **B.A.R.K. Principles** is an excellent foundation for experiencing the parks with your dogs. B.A.R.K. stands for:

B - Bag your pet's waste

A - Always leash your pet

R - Respect Wildlife

K - Know where you can go

Bagging your pet's waste is essential to keep the parks and campgrounds nice for other visitors and prevent parasites and diseases from being passed from your pet to wildlife.

Keeping your pet on a leash serves many purposes in a national park. No matter how well-trained your dog is off-leash, they can easily get overstimulated or distracted by new smells and wildlife. Unleashed dogs are at risk of chasing, harassing, and even injuring or killing wildlife, causing damage to natural features, scaring and disrupting other park visitors, as well as getting lost and injuring themselves. For your and your pet's safety, they must always be on a leash when out of the vehicle, camper, or kennel. The leash cannot exceed 6 feet in length, and it is prohibited to leave dogs tethered outside unattended.

Respecting wildlife has many considerations. Keeping your pet leashed to prevent chasing, harassing, and killing wildlife is just the start. Domestic pets are also at risk of getting or giving diseases to wildlife. Many examples exist of wildlife in parks dying from diseases they have been given by pets and humans. For instance, heartworms from dogs and cats can kill wildlife such as foxes, wolves, coyotes, bobcats, and mountain lions. If humans are sick with the flu and get too close to black-footed ferrets, they can die from the illness. Wolves can be infected by canine parvovirus from dogs. Keeping your pets vaccinated can keep them and wildlife safe. It is also important to keep pet food confined. Do not leave pet food outside vehicles or campers, nor leave a pet dish unattended. It becomes problematic if wild animals learn to visit campgrounds and picnic areas in search of both human and pet food. Certain animals in certain parks may have to be relocated or even euthanized if the hunt for human and pet food becomes a danger to themselves and visitors.

Knowing where you can go is essential for your safety, the safety of your pet and wildlife, and for your enjoyment. It also allows you to make alternative arrangements ahead of time if the circumstances prevent you from enjoying the park the way you would like. Knowing where you can go before you go allows you to prepare for the weather conditions and recreational restrictions and have the necessary documents to board your dog while visiting the park.

You know your pet best. What are they going to be comfortable with? Are they inclined to chase wildlife? Are they friendly with other people and dogs? Are they comfortable in new environments and on trails? Are they easily over-stimulated? Do they tend to eat anything and everything within reach? These are all things to consider when you take your pet to a new situation or environment, including the National Parks. Sometimes, it is more comfortable and enjoyable for you and your pet to board them or make other arrangements.

It is not recommended to leave pets in vehicles for various reasons. The biggest reason is that in hot weather, the heat in the vehicle can quickly become dangerous for the health and life of your pets, even if the windows are opened slightly. It may be tempting to leave your pet in the car to do a quick hike or check out an attraction; however, consider the outside temperature and use the following guide to consider if it is safe to leave your pet in the car even for a short amount of time.

CAR TEMPERATURE
PET SAFETY CHART

IF IT'S THIS HOT OUTSIDE:	IT'S THIS HOT IN YOUR CAR:	
	10 minutes	30 minutes
70°	89°	104°
75°	94°	109°
80°	99°	114°
85°	104°	119°
90°	109°	124°
95°	114°	129°

Within minutes interior car temperatures can be deadly

It is recommended to seek out alternative options before entering the park if the heat or other factors are a concern. Depending on your trip plans, there are usually some boarding options outside the parks, with options for doggie daycare or overnight stays. You will need proof of all vaccinations to provide the boarding facility, so it is best to keep digital copies that can be emailed or copies in the vehicle with you for last-minute boarding during your trip.

Service Animals

The National Park Service revised the policy regarding the use of service animals in 2018. The policy aligns with the standards established by the Department of Justice and the Americans with Disabilities Act.

Service animals are allowed to go wherever visitors are permitted. Service dogs are dogs that have been trained to perform specific tasks that assist a person with a disability or a medical issue. Service animals are working animals and are not considered pets.

According to the Americans with Disabilities Act (ADA), animals that are considered emotional support, therapy, or companion animals (of any type) are not service animals. Emotional support animals are considered pets, not service dogs, and must follow the policies and regulations for pets. Service dogs that are currently in training and not assisting a person with disabilities are also not yet considered service dogs and must abide by the pet regulations.

For more information on the policy regarding service animals in National Parks, please visit: https://www.nps.gov/subjects/accessibility/service-animals.htm

Trail Etiquette (*with Pets*)

- **Pack it in, pack it out:** Anything that comes with you on a trail should leave with you. This includes food, food and drink packaging, and human and pet waste.
- **Proper disposal of human and pet waste:** in national parks or any natural area, human and pet waste must be disposed of appropriately for the enjoyment of others and the safety of wildlife. Human and pet waste can contain bacteria and other things that can make wildlife sick and introduce illnesses that can harm entire herds and packs. Dogs can carry diseases such as parvovirus, giardia, and roundworms into the park and infect wildlife populations. Feces may also pollute water sources.
- **Follow the National Park Service pet leash policy.** Pets in national parks must be leashed and under control at all times so they are not able to chase or harass wildlife.
- **Right of Way:** Wildlife has the right of way in a national park. It is their home. This can sometimes create delays or a need to turn back on a trail for safety reasons. Horses and their riders also have the right of way. Please move to the side of the trail and keep pets under control while horses and stock animals pass on the trail. If your pet is not pet, animal, or human friendly, let others with or without pets pass while you step out of the way. Not everyone is comfortable around dogs; please be considerate. Hikers coming uphill have the right of way over hikers traveling downhill.
- **Stay on the trail.** Stepping off the trail can damage plants and animal species and have a negative effect on the ecosystem. If you must step off the trail, such as to yield to the

right of way, try to follow the principle of Leave No Trace and step where little to no damage can be done.

· **Consider trail and weather conditions.** Inclement weather can create dangerously slippery trail conditions, and hiking on muddy trails can damage trail conditions or the ecosystem surrounding the trail.

· **Make yourself known to other hikers and wildlife.** While many enjoy the quiet peace that comes from hiking, it is courteous to let other hikers know of your presence and alert wildlife to your presence, creating a safer environment for you and the wildlife.

· **Be sure to listen.** While it is safe and considerate to alert other hikers and wildlife of your presence as needed, it is best not to have a constant noise source, such as music on a portable speaker. It is also not recommended to wear headphones while in the wild. Being able to listen allows you to hear any potential dangers ahead or approaching noises.

· **Be aware of your surroundings when hiking, especially in new locations.** Each park has its own unique landscape and variety of wildlife that can create a different hiking experience. Research ahead of time or stop by a ranger station or visitor center to ask about specific risks involved with hiking in new and unfamiliar locations such as temperatures, snakes, insects, diseases, etc.

The 10+ Essentials for Hiking (*with Pets*)

1. **Navigation** - Map, compass, and GPS. Be sure to know how to use these tools before you hit the trail. There may not always be cell service in the National Parks, especially on backcountry trails.
2. **Water** - Ensure you have enough water for yourself and your pet, appropriate for the weather conditions. The higher the temps, the more water is needed.
3. **Food** - Bring lunch and snacks beyond what you think you may want or need. Keeping some granola bars, trail mix, nuts, and dried fruit works well to keep on hand and give you a little boost if needed.
4. **Layers** - Temperatures can start low and rise considerably throughout the day and drop drastically again at night once the sun goes down; it is best to bring layers to accommodate different temperatures throughout your hike easily. Consider items such as rain jackets, packable down jackets, gloves, and hats depending on the area, climate, and landscape where you will be hiking.
5. **Light** - Flashlights and headlamps are necessary for overnight trips but can also become incredibly useful if your day hike goes a little later than expected. Due to trees and mountains, it can become pretty dark even before sunset.
6. **Sun Protection** - Some trails may not provide much shade, so it is best to bring sunscreen, sunglasses, hats, and possibly even long pants and long sleeves to avoid sunburn.
7. **Fire** - Waterproof matches, lighters, and other fire-starters. Being able to start a fire can aid in cooking, staying warm, or use as an emergency notification.

8. **First-Aid Supplies** - Small packable first-aid kits can be purchased, modified, and refilled as needed. Consider what you might need if you or your pet gets any cuts or scrapes.
9. **Tools** - A multi-tool is a compact way to come prepared with almost anything you may need, including a knife, pliers, wire cutters, etc.
10. **Emergency Shelter** - Bring a space blanket, small tarp, bivy sack, or something that can separate you from possible inclement weather.
11. **Waste Removal** - Both human and pet waste should never be left on, along, or off the trail in natural areas, not only for the enjoyment of other hikers but also because it poses health risks to wildlife. All solid human waste, feminine hygiene products, toilet paper, and things used as toilet paper, must be carried out in a landfill-safe commercial toilet bag. Pet waste must also be appropriately bagged and deposited in trash receptacles.

https://www.nps.gov/articles/10essentials.htm

4

Become a B.A.R.K. Ranger

In the last chapter, we introduced the B.A.R.K. Principles as a foundation for responsibly visiting National Parks with dogs. In addition to the principles that are universal for all National Parks that allow dogs, some individual parks have a B.A.R.K. Ranger program. The program is not currently available in every park, but it is available in the parks listed below and some of the other Park Service areas, such as National and Historical Monument areas.

B.A.R.K. stands for:
- **B** - Bag your pet's waste
- **A** - Always leash your pet
- **R** - Respect Wildlife
- **K** - Know where you can go

The B.A.R.K. Ranger Program is part of the Healthy People Healthy Parks Initiative from the National Park Service. The parks listed below have started their own B.A.R.K. Ranger programs. The program is all about exploring, learning, and protecting national parks. You will learn how to be safe and take care of the park while visiting with your dog by following the B.A.R.K. guidelines outlined above.

As of 2023, the following National Parks have a B.A.R.K. Ranger Program:

Please note: Pets are not allowed in federal buildings (36 CFR 2.15), including visitor centers. Please inquire about the B.A.R.K. Ranger programs without your pets and follow the instructions of each program.

Acadia National Park (Maine) – Visit the campground ranger station, the Sieur de Monts Nature Center, or the Hulls Cove Visitor Center to pick up a copy of an activity checklist and learn more about Acadia's Bark Ranger program. After completing this short program, dogs can be sworn in as B.A.R.K. Rangers. A special collar tag unique to Acadia will be available for purchase to official B.A.R.K. Rangers at the Eastern National Bookstore at the Hulls Cove Visitor Center.

Biscayne National Park (Florida) – Visit the Dante Fascell Visitor Center for a B.A.R.K. Ranger activity booklet. Once you complete the activities, collect a badge that can be attached to a collar, leash, or harness.

Bryce Canyon National Park (Utah) – Stop by the visitor center for an official B.A.R.K. Ranger card and a dog treat. B.A.R.K. Ranger pet tags and patches are also available for purchase in the Bryce Canyon Natural History Association Bookstore located in the visitor center.

Gateway Arch National Park (Missouri) - Stop by the visitor center entrance desk to get a B.A.R.K. Ranger booklet and receive a free award. Visit the website for upcoming B.A.R.K. Ranger events: https://www.nps.gov/jeff/planyourvisit/pets.htm

Great Smoky Mountains National Park (North Carolina & Tennessee) - Stop by a Visitor Center to ask about their B.A.R.K. Ranger program. The Great Smoky Mountains Association has B.A.R.K. Ranger products, such as a collapsible bowl, a leash, and a collar tag available for purchase.

Hawai'i Volcanoes National Park (Hawai'i) - Take the B.A.R.K. Ranger pledge, download and fill out the B.A.R.K. Ranger Certificate, and bring it into the Kīlauea Visitor Center to have it officially stamped. You can then take your stamped certificate to the Hawai'i Pacific Parks Association store, where Bark Ranger dog tags and Bark Ranger bandanas can be purchased with proceeds supporting the park. https://www.nps.gov/havo/planyourvisit/pets.htm

Hot Springs National Park (Arkansas) - Visit the Fordyce Bathhouse and Visitor Center to discuss the B.A.R.K. Ranger Program with a ranger. Completing two designated activities on the B.A.R.K. Ranger activity card within the park will satisfy the program requirements. Successful dogs will be sworn in as official B.A.R.K. Rangers and get a certificate of completion. Dogs are not allowed in the visitor center, but well-behaved dogs are allowed on the front porch, where water is provided.

Indiana Dunes National Park (Indiana) - Stop by the visitor center, Paul H. Douglas Center, or on a BARK Ranger hike to get an activity booklet. After taking the pledge, you can get a dog tag for a $5 donation to Friends of Indiana Dunes. Indiana Dunes National Park also has a B.A.R.K. Ranger Ambassador Program. More information can be found at: https://www.nps.gov/indu/planyourvisit/bark-rangers.htm

New River Gorge National Park (West Virginia) - Visit any visitor center to take the B.A.R.K. Ranger pledge. You will receive a signed certificate and tag for your dog's collar as an official New River Gorge B.A.R.K. Ranger!

Olympic National Park (Washington) - Visit the Kalaloch Ranger Station to participate.

Petrified Forest National Park (Arizona) - Stop by the visitor center for an official B.A.R.K. Ranger card and a dog treat. B.A.R.K. Ranger pet tags are also available for purchase at the visitor centers.

Petrified Forest National Park (Arizona) - Ask about the program at any park entrance booth or the Visitor Center to get a card with all the program info. Your pet will get a treat and B.A.R.K. Ranger pet tags are available for purchase at Visitor Centers.

Redwood National Park (California) - Visit any of the visitor centers to take the B.A.R.K. Ranger Pledge and get a stamped certificate. B.A.R.K. Rangers can purchase a Redwood exclusive dog collar tag at the Redwood Parks Conservancy bookstores. For more information and to get the Redwood National Park BARK! Ranger brochure, visit: https://www.nps.gov/redw/planyourvisit/pets.htm

Wrangell-St. Elias (Alaska) - Please contact the visitor's center to inquire about specific program details.

Yosemite National Park (California) - Visit any visitor center to get an official B.A.R.K. Ranger pledge card.

If your favorite park is not listed above, please visit or call the park's visitor center to inquire if they currently have a B.A.R.K. Ranger program.

5

The Most Dog-Friendly National Parks

In this chapter, you will be introduced to the National Parks with the most pet access. Parks are listed in alphabetical order, not in order of most access, to make finding the park you are interested in quicker and easier. Following the park name in parenthesis are the state(s) in which it is located and the year it was established as a National Park.

Most of these parks still have limited access. While we intend to provide the most accurate and up-to-date information at the time of writing and publication, it is always advised to visit the website (links provided) or inquire at the visitor center regarding the most current pet access. Doing this will ensure you have the most up-to-date information on closed trails, seasonally protected areas, and other closures. It will also provide notification of any potential health risks that may affect your pet. This book is meant to be a quick and easy offline guide and supplement to aid in preparation and planning enjoyable visits to the National Parks, but we cannot guarantee that the information, access, and restrictions may not change after publication.

The parks in this section allow dogs in areas other than just roadways, parking lots, picnic areas, and drive-in campgrounds.

Acadia National Park (Maine, 1919)

Acadia is mainly located on Mount Desert Island, which is the largest island off the coast of Maine. The park encompasses approximately 50,000 acres along the Atlantic Coastline of Maine, including 60 miles of coastline. There are 33 miles of scenic roads, 45 miles of carriage roads, and over 150 miles of hiking trails to explore within the park. Wildlife is abundant in the park, and sea life is abundant off the shore. Acadia is one of the top ten most visited national parks and is considered the "Crown Jewel of the North."

Pets in Acadia:

Pets are allowed on roads, parking areas, carriage roads, and most trails. Pets are allowed for day hiking only on Isle au Haut. Pets are allowed in Blackwoods, Seawall, and Schoodic Woods campgrounds. The park has 100 miles of hiking trails and 45 miles of early carriage roads where pets are allowed. Pets must be on a leash no longer than 6 feet in length. Pet waste must be collected and deposited in a trash receptacle. Carry pet waste out with you; do not leave it hanging from trees or on the side of the trail. Pets are not allowed in lakes. Most of the lakes in the park are public water supplies, and because of this, pets and people are not allowed to swim in them. Sand Beach and Echo Lake are off-limits to pets from May 15th through October 15th. Pets are not allowed in public buildings or on ranger-led programs. Pets are prohibited in Duck Harbor Campground or the Wild Gardens of Acadia (Sieur de Monte.) Pets are not allowed on the following trails: Beehive, Ladder Trail to Dorr Mountain, Precipice, Beech Cliffs Trail, Perpendicular Trail (Mansell Mountain), and Jordan Cliffs Trail between Penobscot East Trail and the carriage road. The following trails are not recommended for pets: Flying Mountain, Giant Slide, Acadia Mountain, Cadillac Mountain - West face, Bubble and Jordan Ponds Path between the carriage road the Featherbed pond, Bubbles-Pemetic Trail, Norembega Goat Trail, Penobscot Mountain (Spring) Trail, Upper Beachcroft Trail, and Upper Gorge Trail. Pets should not be left unattended in vehicles or at campgrounds.

B.A.R.K. Ranger Park

https://www.nps.gov/articles/be-an-acadia-bark-ranger.ht m

Biscayne National Park (Florida, 1980)

Biscayne is 95% water and is explored primarily by boating, diving, and snorkeling. Biscayne was initially designated as a National Monument in 1968 after conservationists lobbied to protect the site from development and destruction. Biscayne now protects mangrove forests, coral reefs, Biscayne Bay, and 10,000 years of human history. One of the main attractions is the Maritime Heritage Trail, which provides prime snorkeling and diving at six of the park's shipwrecks.

Pets in Biscayne:

Pets are allowed on roadways and in parking areas. Pets are also allowed at Elliott Key and on the grounds at Convoy Point. Pets must be on a leash no longer than 6 feet long and must not be tied to any object and left unattended. Pet waste must be collected and properly disposed of in a trash receptacle. Pets are not allowed in the visitor center or on Boca Chita Key, including on boats docked in the harbor.

*B.A.R.K. Ranger Park

https://www.nps.gov/bisc/planyourvisit/pets.htm

Black Canyon of the Gunnison National Park (Colorado, 1999)

Black Canyon of the Gunnison is named for the dark rock walls that descend into the canyon that was formed by the Gunnison River. Rock in the bottom of this gorge dates back to 1.7 Billion years ago. The Painted Wall is the highest cliff in Colorado and is world-renowned among rock climbers. Black Canyon of the Gunnison National Park is also an International Dark Sky Park, which means it is an excellent place for night sky viewing!

Pets in Black Canyon of the Gunnison:

Pets are allowed in parking lots, picnic areas, campgrounds, paths to overlooks, and along roads that are open to vehicles. Pets are also allowed on the Rim Rock Trail between the campground and South Rim Visitor Center and on the North Rim Chasm View Nature Trail. Well-behaved pets are also allowed at Ranger Programs at the campground amphitheater. Pets are always required to be on a leash, no longer than 6 feet long. Pet waste must be picked up immediately and may not be left to pick up later. Owners are responsible for their pets and may receive fines if their animal creates problems with wildlife and other visitors. Pets are not allowed on any hiking trails not listed above, on designated cross-country ski or snowshoe trails, in the inner canyon wilderness, or anywhere else in the park.

https://www.nps.gov/blca/planyourvisit/pets2.htm

Bryce Canyon National Park (Utah, 1928)

Bryce Canyon was initially established as Bryce Canyon National Monument in 1923 and was administered by the U. S. Forest Service. In 1924, it became Utah National Park and joined the National Park Service. It was in 1928 that it became Bryce Canyon National Park as we know it today. The canyon, and later the park, was named after an area rancher, Ebenezer Bryce, who was tracking down his livestock. Locals began calling the area "Bryce's Canyon" after his discovery. Of course, Bryce was not the first human to come across this area, as Native Americans had been in the area for centuries prior. Bryce Canyon is most well known for the unique landscape and red rock formations referred to as "hoodoos," which were created over thousands of years of freezing and erosion.

Pets in Bryce Canyon:
    Pets are only allowed on paved surfaces in the park, including

roads, viewpoints (except Piracy Point,) parking lots, and drive-in campgrounds. Pets are also allowed on the Rim Trail between Sunset Point and Sunrise Point and the Shared Use Path between the park entrance and Inspiration Point. Pets are not permitted on trails, in buildings, or on public transportation. This policy applies to pets that are carried without exception.

B.A.R.K. Ranger Park

https://www.nps.gov/brca/planyourvisit/pets.htm

Capitol Reef National Park (Utah, 1971)

Capitol Reef features a geologic monocline, a wrinkle on the earth's surface, extending approximately 100 miles. This unique feature is called Waterpocket Fold. This park is in the south-central part of the state and features the red rocks for which this area is known in Utah. In addition to Waterpocket Fold, the park boasts cliffs, canyons, domes, and bridges. The park is also an International Dark Sky Park as of 2015.

Pets in Capitol Reef:
    Pets are allowed in parking areas open to public vehicles, drive-in campgrounds, and within 50 feet of the centerline of both paved and dirt roads open to public travel. Pets are also allowed in the Chestnut and Doc Inglesby picnic areas, in unfenced and unlocked orchards, on the Fremont River trail from the campground to the south end of Hatties Field (where there is a gate), and on the trail from the visitor center to the Fruita

24

Campground. Pets are required to be on a leash no longer than 6 feet at all times. Pets are not allowed on hiking trails that aren't listed above, in the backcountry, or in public buildings.

B.A.R.K. Ranger Park

https://www.nps.gov/care/planyourvisit/pets.htm

Crater Lake National Park (Oregon, 1902)

Crater Lake was created approximately 7,700 years ago when the Mount Mazama volcano erupted so violently that it blew the top off the peak. After this eruption, Mount Mazama could no longer support its own weight, causing it to collapse in on itself, creating the caldera that has been collecting snowfall and rainwater for centuries. This event created the deepest lake in the United States and one of the world's most pristine waters due to the water's purity. There are hiking and boating opportunities in the park, and in the winter, activities include cross-country skiing and snowshoeing.

Pets in Crater Lake:

Pets are allowed on paved roads and within 50 feet of the paved surfaces, in parking areas and paved walkways, in all picnic areas, and in the Mazama and Lost Creek campgrounds. Pets are also allowed on the following trails: Lady of the Woods and Godfrey Glen as long as there is not a significant amount of snow; the Annie Spur Trail, which connects the Pacific Crest Trail to Mazama Village; Grayback Drive when East Rim Drive is open, and the official portions of the Pacific Crest Trail (P.C.T.) within the park. In the Summer and Fall, the paved promenade in Rim Village is a great place to walk the dog, with views of the lake. In the Winter and Spring, the Rim Village parking lot is the best place to walk dogs, and pets are allowed on paved roads and in parking lots free of significant snow. Dogs are allowed on the Pacific Crest Trail year-round, regardless of snow cover. Pets are not permitted on Cleetwood Cove Trail, in the wilderness areas, in any bodies of water in the park, including Crater Lake, or in park buildings. Pets are prohibited on any hiking trails or designated ski routes except those listed above.

https://www.nps.gov/crla/planyourvisit/pets.htm

Congaree National Park (South Carolina, 2003)

Congaree protects the largest remaining expanse of old-growth bottomland hardwood forest in the southeastern United States. The Congaree River Blue Trail provides a unique experience and access to the park. It is a 50-mile designated recreational paddling trail, extending from the state capital of Columbia downstream to the national park. Once in the park, paddlers can take out of the water and explore the park's 20 miles of established hiking trails. In addition to paddling and hiking, visitors to the park can also enjoy backpacking, camping, fishing, and birding.

Pets in Congaree:
    Pets are allowed on all public roadways, in parking lots, picnic

areas, and campgrounds. Pets are allowed on all trails in the park and in boats on the water. Pets are not allowed in park buildings. Pets must be on a leash no longer than 6 feet in length, and pet waste must be collected and deposited in a trash receptacle.

https://www.nps.gov/cong/planyourvisit/pets.htm

Cuyahoga Valley National Park (Ohio, 2000)

Cuyahoga Valley contains the winding Cuyahoga River. The most popular trail in the park is the Towpath Trail, which follows the historic route of the Ohio and Erie Canal. Visitors can enjoy the park by hiking, biking, boating, horseback, and even by taking a scenic train ride. The park is open all year and has winter recreation and activities to enjoy, including cross-country skiing, sledding, snowshoeing, and ice fishing.

Pets in Cuyahoga Valley:
   Pets are allowed on over 100 miles of the over 125 miles of hiking trails as well as on the multi-use Towpath Trail. Pets are not allowed on the Cuyahoga Valley Scenic Railroad or the East Rim mountain bike trails. Pets are not allowed in park buildings. Pets are prohibited at Virginia Kendall Hills during sledding activities. Pets must be on a leash no longer than 6 feet, and pet waste must be collected and deposited in trash receptacles.

https://www.nps.gov/cuva/planyourvisit/pets.htm

Denali National Park & Preserve (Alaska, 1917)

Denali Park is home to North America's tallest peak, Denali, at 20,310 feet, and an abundance of wildlife. Denali was the first park created to protect wildlife, which includes 39 species of mammals such as moose, grizzly bears, caribou, and wolves, 169 species of birds, and one amphibian species. That lone amphibian is the Wood Frog, and it can survive the harsh winter temperatures because it has adapted to freezing solid during the winter months.

Pets in Denali:

Dogs are permitted in the park with the standard restrictions of being on leash and allowed on park roads, parking lots, and in campgrounds. Dogs are not allowed off-leash, off-trail, or on park trails, except for the Roadside Trail and the Bike Path, which dogs are allowed on leash. While dogs can be in your private vehicle, private vehicles are only allowed to enter a short distance into the park. To fully experience Denali and have the greatest chance of seeing the vast wildlife the park has to offer, it is best to take a bus further into the park. Pets are not allowed on the buses, so it might be best to make other arrangements so you can make the most of your trip into Denali.

https://www.nps.gov/dena/planyourvisit/pets.htm

Dry Tortugas National Park (Florida, 1992)

Dry Tortugas is located almost 70 miles west of Key West. The park consists of seven small islands; the rest is open water. The park boasts beautiful blue waters, coral reefs, and marine life. Garden Key is home to Fort Jefferson, "Guardian of the Gulf," intended to protect the harbor and waterway, and was one of the largest forts ever built. Construction began in 1846 and continued until 1875, but was never finished or fully armed. The fort was used during the Civil War by Union troops and then abandoned by the army in 1874. It was used briefly during both world wars, and now it is a protected piece of history in the park that visitors can explore.

Pets in Dry Tortugas:
   Pets are allowed on Garden Key. Pets are required to be on a leash no longer than 6 feet in length at all times, and pet waste must be collected and disposed of in a trash receptacle. Pets are not allowed inside Fort Jefferson. Pets are not allowed on any other key in the park. Please note that the only way to get to the park is by boat or seaplane. The commercial ferry and seaplane do not allow pets on board. Visitors arriving by personal boat or by permitted tour guides are welcome to bring pets.

https://www.nps.gov/drto/planyourvisit/pets.htm

Gates of the Arctic National Park & Preserve (Alaska, 1980)

Gates of the Arctic National Park is located in the northernmost region of the Rocky Mountains, north of the Arctic Circle. The area consists of remote wilderness, rugged mountains, rivers, lakes, and wildlife. It is the second largest wilderness area in the National Park Service, consisting of 7,523,897 acres in the National Park portion and 948,608 acres when combined with the two units that make up the preserve. The park has no roads, entrance gates, or visitor centers. The land has been used and has been home to Alaska Native people for over ten thousand years and continues to be a source of sustenance and recreation. It is important to respect not only the land but also the culture and the valuable resources the land and ecosystem provide.

Pets in Gates of the Arctic:

There are no restricted areas to pets in the park. However, as required by law in all national parks, pets must be confined or restrained at all times and on a leash no longer than 6 feet in length. This policy helps ensure pet safety by preventing them from becoming lost or injured, prevent them from harassing wildlife or causing predation, endangering other visitors, or damaging resources. It is important to acknowledge that pets can attract wildlife and create dangerous situations for wildlife, pets, and their owners. It is illegal and punishable if an unrestrained pet kills wildlife or disrupts the natural process of animals in the park. Due to the remote aspect of the park, it may be easier to leave your dogs at home or board them while visiting this park.

https://www.nps.gov/gaar/planyourvisit/pets.htm

Gateway Arch National Park (Missouri, 2018)

Gateway Arch is one of the few national parks in an urban area and protects history, not just wild landscapes, wildlife, and unique natural features. Construction of the arch began in 1963 and was completed in 1965. Both the north and south trams were completed by 1968. The 630-foot tall arch was intended to be a symbol of Thomas Jefferson's vision of creating a unified continental nation with the American West during the 19th Century. Both St. Louis and the arch are referred to as the "Gateway to the West." The park was formerly named Jefferson National Expansion Memorial before it recently became designated as a national park. The park also encompasses St. Louis' "Old Courthouse," where the Dred Scott v. Sandford case was held. The Dred Scott case is considered one of the most important cases ever tried in the United States because of the role it played in hastening the Civil War, which led to the freedom of enslaved people. (Please note that the old courthouse is closed for renovations at the time of writing. Visit the park website for current status and reopening.)

Pets in Gateway Arch:

Pets are allowed in all outdoor areas of the park. Pets must be on a leash no longer than 6 feet in length. Pets are not allowed to go in the reflecting pools or garden beds. Pets are not allowed in any buildings. Do not leave your pet tied to objects and left unattended. Gateway not only has a B.A.R.K. Ranger program, but they also have B.A.R.K. Ranger events just for the pets, including a Halloween Costume Parade! Please visit the website for current and upcoming events.

* B.A.R.K. Ranger Park

https://www.nps.gov/jeff/planyourvisit/pets.htm

Grand Canyon National Park (Arizona, 1919)

Grand Canyon is one of the most dynamic examples of erosions in the world. Approximately 278 miles of the Colorado River cuts through the canyon, creating one of the seven natural wonders of the world known as the Grand Canyon. The park also encompasses the ancestral homeland of 11 associated tribes. The park has many recreational opportunities, from viewing the canyon from the many overlooks, rim trail hiking, below-the-rim hiking, rafting the Colorado River, and mule rides. Due to the high elevation at the top of the rim, the Grand Canyon receives snowfall in the winter. The South Rim remains open year-round.

Pets in Grand Canyon:

Pets are allowed at the South Rim on above-rim trails, in Mather Campground, Desert View Campground, Trailer Village, and developed areas. Yavapai Lodge is the only in-park lodge that has pet-friendly rooms. There are also kennels inside the park if you would like to venture below the rim or take a mule ride. (See website for kennel information and requirements.) At the North Rim, pets are only allowed on the bridle (greenway) trail that connects the North Kaibab Trail and the portion of the Arizona Trail north to the park entrance station. At Tuweep, pets are only allowed on established roads and in the campground. Pets are not allowed on any trails below the rim, in the backcountry, on park shuttle buses, or in any public buildings other than pet-friendly rooms.

https://www.nps.gov/grca/planyourvisit/pets.htm

Great Basin National Park (Nevada, 1986)

Great Basin National Park is part of the greater Great Basin Region. The park protects groves of bristlecone pines, some of the oldest trees on earth, with one tree cut down in 1964, estimated to be around 4,900 years old. The park has at least 42 caves, with tours of Lehman Caves available to the public. The park also hosts an annual astronomy festival.

Pets in Great Basin:
  Pets are allowed on roads, drive-in campgrounds, and in parking lots. Pets are also allowed on the Lexington Arch Trail and the trail between Baker and the Great Basin Visitor Center. Pets are not allowed on any other trails or in the wilderness areas. Pets are not permitted in the caves or at evening programs. They are not allowed in park buildings. Tethering a pet to trees or other fixtures and leaving them unattended is prohibited. All pet waste must be collected and disposed of in a trash bin or dumpster.

https://www.nps.gov/grba/planyourvisit/pets.htm

Great Sand Dunes National Park (Colorado, 2004)

Great Sand Dunes encompass the tallest dunes in North America. Star Dune, the highest in the park, reaches 755 feet tall. It is not just sand dunes; the park also encompasses a diverse landscape of grasslands, wetlands, forests, alpine lakes, and tundra. Activities in the park include sandboarding and sand sledding, hiking and backpacking, horseback riding, and more. Great Sand Dunes is also an International Dark Sky Park, which makes it a great place to view the night sky, especially when it is not a full moon.

Pets in Great Sand Dunes:
   Pets are allowed on paved roads, parking lots, and primary use areas of the park, including Piñon Flats Campground, Dunes Overlook Trail, and along the Medano Pass Primitive Road. Pets are allowed in the Preserve, including the Mosca Pass Trail. Pets must be on a leash at all times when outside of vehicles. Pets are not allowed inside the visitor center or bathrooms, in the backcountry of the dune field beyond the first high ridge of the dunes, or off the Dunes Overlook Trail. Pets are also not allowed north of Castle Creek Picnic Area, except along Medano Pass Primitive Road. Pets are not permitted north of Point of No Return, including on Sand Ramp Trail. Pets are not permitted in any backpacking campsites within the park. Please visit the website for maps showing where pets are and are not permitted within the park. More detailed information can also be found on the website regarding park-specific safety concerns for pets and laws and fines pertaining to pets within the park.

https://www.nps.gov/grsa/planyourvisit/pets.htm

Great Smoky Mountains National Park (North Carolina & Tennessee, 1934)

Great Smoky Mountains is America's most visited national park, with over nine million people visiting annually. There are ten front country campgrounds as well as backcountry camping options to accommodate visitors. The park has over 800 miles of hiking trails, including a portion of the Appalachian Trail. It is estimated that approximately 1,900 black bears live in the Great Smoky Mountains, along with a wide variety of wildlife, including 65 species of mammals, 80 different reptiles and amphibians, over 200 types of birds, and 67 native fish. In addition to the park, there are many tourist attractions surrounding the park, including Dollywood, which is just 10 miles outside the park.

Pets in the Great Smoky Mountains:
   Pets are allowed along roads, in parking areas, picnic areas, and campgrounds. Pets are also allowed on two short walking paths: the Gatlinburg Trail and the Oconaluftee River Trail. Pets are prohibited on all other trails in the park. Pets must always be on a leash when outside vehicles and R.V.s. Pet waste must be collected immediately and disposed of in a trash receptacle. Pets should not be left unattended in vehicles or R.V.s at campsites.

* B.A.R.K. Ranger Park

https://www.nps.gov/grsm/planyourvisit/pets.htm

Guadalupe Mountains National Park (Texas, 1972)

Guadalupe Mountains contains the four highest peaks in Texas, as well as mountains, canyons, deserts, and dunes. The Salt Basin has dunes up to 60 feet tall made from white gypsum and pale red quartz. The park also protects the world's most extensive Permian fossil reef. The park has 80 miles of hiking trails, including the trail up to Guadalupe Peak, which climbs 3000 feet. Hiking and backpacking are popular activities in Texas's largest designated wilderness area.

Pets in Guadalupe Mountains:
   Pets are allowed in areas that are accessible by motor vehicles, such as established roads and roadsides, parking areas, and developed picnic areas and campgrounds. Pets are also allowed on the Pine Springs Campground Connector Trail and the Pinery Trail from the visitor center to the Butterfield Stage Station. Pets must be on a leash no longer than 6 feet at all times when outside of a vehicle. Federal regulations require all pet waste to be picked up and disposed of in a trash receptacle. Pets are not allowed in park buildings or restrooms, at public ranger programs, in the backcountry, and on trails other than the ones listed above.

https://www.nps.gov/gumo/planyourvisit/pets.htm

Hot Springs National Park (Arkansas, 1921)

Hot Springs is unique because although its main feature is a natural wonder, the hot spring water itself, the park is also a cultural and medical historical site. It is also one of the few national parks that exists in an urban setting, situated in the town of Hot Springs, Arkansas. There are eight historic bathhouses lined up on "Bathhouse Row" that were constructed between the years of 1892 and 1923. The largest and grandest of the bathhouses is the Fordyce Bathhouse, which is also the Visitor Center and a museum. The museum provides insight into medicine before penicillin and what we now consider modern medicine. The trails behind Bathhouse Row were often part of patients' prescribed treatment for their ailments and are available for you to walk the same paths. Baths are not available in Fordyce, but there are several options for bathing in the hot spring waters in Hot Springs. There are also several taps around town where you can fill water bottles with potable water from the springs.

Pets in Hot Springs:

Pets are allowed in all areas of the park, with the exception of the federal buildings. Pets must be on a leash at all times inside the park. Pet waste stations are at each end of Bathhouse Row and the campground. Pets are allowed on all 26 miles of trails inside the park and in the Superior Bathhouse Restaurant and Brewery. Areas that are closed to park visitors, such as the thermal springs, are off-limits. Pets and people may not swim in them.

*B.A.R.K. Ranger Park

37

https://www.nps.gov/hosp/planyourvisit/pets.htm

Indiana Dunes National Park (Indiana, 2019)

Indiana Dunes consists of 15 miles of shoreline along Lake Michigan. The recently designated national park was previously Indiana Dune National Lakeshore. There is a hiking challenge called the 1966 Hiking Challenge, which includes 19 hikes consisting of 66 miles of trails in the park. Another hiking challenge is the Diana of the Dunes Dare, which incorporates history and local lore. And if you complete the challenge, you can collect a sticker as a badge of honor. The park is open year-round, and in addition to hiking, popular activities include swimming, biking, bird watching, camping, boating, and horseback riding. If you are visiting in September, you may also want to check out the Outdoor Adventure Festival, which overlaps with the Duneland Fall Festival.

Pets in Indiana Dunes:

Pets are allowed on public roadways and parking areas. Pets are allowed on the Pinhook Upland Trail. They are allowed on all beaches, except for the lifeguarded swimming area at West Beach, from the Friday of Memorial Day Weekend through the Monday of Labor Day Weekend. Pets must be on a leash no longer than 6 feet at all times, even when swimming in the lake. Pet owners allowing pets to chase birds or otherwise harass wildlife are subject to a citation. All pet waste must be collected and deposited into proper trash receptacles. Pets are not allowed on the Pinhook Bog Trail, Glenwood Dune Trail, the nature play areas, or in any park buildings. Areas may be subject to temporary pet restrictions and will be posted.

B.A.R.K. Ranger Park

https://www.nps.gov/indu/planyourvisit/pets.htm

Mammoth Cave National Park (Kentucky, 1941)

Mammoth Cave is notable for being the world's longest-known cave system. However, cave tours aren't the only things to do in the park. The park covers over 52,000 acres in south-central Kentucky and provides recreational hiking, horseback riding, boating, and camping opportunities. In addition to the cave's rich history, there are also historic churches and cemeteries in the park. The park is also designated as a UNESCO World Heritage Site and International Biosphere Reserve.

Pets in Mammoth Cave:

Pets are allowed on roads, parking areas, and on all surface trails in the park. The Woodland Cottages have pet-friendly rooms in the park. Pets must be on a leash at all times, and pet waste must be collected and properly disposed of in trash receptacles. Pets are not allowed in the caves or in park buildings. Hikers may encounter horseback riders on trails; hikers and their pets should move to the side of the trail and keep pets under control as horses pass.

https://www.nps.gov/maca/planyourvisit/pets.htm

Mesa Verde National Park (Colorado, 1906)

Mesa Verde was the first park created to protect a location of cultural significance. The park contains and protects nearly 5,000 Puebloan (formerly Anasazi) archaeological sites, including 600 cliff dwellings and the cultural heritage of 26 Pueblos and Tribes. It is estimated that humans inhabited the dwellings for around 700 years, and why they left the area is unknown. The dwellings were never used again and were considered sacred by the Ute. In 1888, a couple of farmers came across the ruins. In 1906, in order to stop the theft of artifacts and destruction that was taking place at the sites, President Theodore Roosevelt signed the Antiquities Act of 1906. A few weeks later, the area officially became a protected area when it was designated as a National Park. The park is also a World Heritage Site and an International Dark Sky Park. In addition to the rich cultural aspect of the park, it is also home to over a thousand species, including several that do not exist anywhere else on Earth.

Pets in Mesa Verde:
  Pets are allowed on paved roads, in parking lots, and drive-in campgrounds. Pets are allowed on some paved trails in the Park Point and the Mesa Top Loop sites and in the park headquarters area. Pets are also allowed on most Wetherill Mesa trails, except the Step House Trail, including the Long House Loop, Badger House Community, and Nordenskiöld Site #16 Trail. Pets are not allowed in park buildings, inside ancestral sites, most overlooks, and on most park trails. Pets must be leashed at all times outside of vehicles. Pets must not be tethered or left unattended.

https://www.nps.gov/meve/planyourvisit/visiting-with-pets.

htm

New River Gorge National Park & Preserve (West Virginia, 2020)

New River Gorge encompasses over 70,000 acres of land along the New River, which, despite its name and being part of the most recent additions to the National Park System, the river is considered one of the oldest rivers on the continent. The park provides many recreational opportunities, including camping, hiking, biking, climbing, white water rafting, fishing, and guided activities with park rangers. In addition to recreational activities, the park has cultural attractions such as the railroad and coal mining towns of Thurmond, Prince, and Nuttallburg. Visitors may also look into early subsistence farming at the Richmond Hamilton Farm and Trump-Lilly Farm. Another unique park offering is the self-guided African American Heritage Tour, which takes visitors to seventeen historic sites that tell the stories of the black coal miners, railroad workers, and other community members who helped shape the region.

Pets in New River Gorge:
   Pets are allowed on roads, parking areas, and anywhere a public vehicle is allowed. Pets are also allowed on all trails as long as they are on a leash no longer than 6 feet long. Pet waste must be collected and deposited in a trash receptacle. Pets are not allowed in park buildings, including the visitor centers. Pets are not allowed at ranger-led programs.

B.A.R.K. Ranger Park

https://www.nps.gov/neri/planyourvisit/bark-ranger.htm

Olympic National Park (Washington, 1938)

Olympic National Park encompasses a diverse landscape of wilderness, old-growth temperate rainforest, mountains, glaciers, and over 70 miles of coastline. The park is home to wildlife such as deer, elk, cougars, and bears. The waters are home to the spawning runs of five different salmon species and are some of the healthiest runs outside of Alaska. There are whales, dolphins, seals, sea lions, porpoises, and sea otters offshore.

Pets in Olympic:

Pets are allowed in drive-in campgrounds, picnic areas, and paved or dirt roads on leash. They are also allowed on the following trails: Peabody Creek Trail (Olympic National Park Visitor Center in Port Angeles), Rialto Beach parking lot to Ellen Creek (1/2 mile), the beaches between the Hoh and Quinault Reservations (Kalaloch area), Madison Falls Trail (Elwha), Spruce Railroad Trail (North shore of Lake Crescent), and the July Creek Loop Trail (North shore of Lake Quinault). Pets are not allowed on any trails not listed above, in public buildings, on interpretive walks, or in the wilderness areas. Pets should not be allowed on tidal rocks due to the risk of stones, shells, and barnacles cutting their paws, which can lead to infection. Do not allow pets to dig or roll in plants, causing harm to the vegetation. Pets are not to be left unattended, as they can attract predatory wildlife.

B.A.R.K. Ranger Park

https://www.nps.gov/olym/planyourvisit/pets.htm

Petrified Forest National Park (Arizona, 1962)

Petrified Forest is best known for its Triassic-period fossils and the world's largest collection of prehistoric petrified wood. The petrified wood features segments of trees that, when living, were over 200 feet tall with trunks up to eight feet in diameter. They were buried over 200 million years ago in volcanic ash that protected the wood from decay and, over time, became the quartz remnants you can see today. In addition to the fossils and petrified wood, there are also remnants of Native American rock art and Puerto Pueblo ruins, a 100-plus room community.

Pets in Petrified Forest:

Pets are allowed on any paved road or trail. Petrified Forest is one of the few parks that also allows pets in designated wilderness areas of the park. All types of pets are welcome in Petrified Forest but must be leashed, contained, or otherwise controlled, just as our dogs. There is even a fenced dog park, The Petrified Forest Bark Park, located next to the parking lot for the Painted Desert Visitor Center. Pets are not allowed in park buildings.

* B.A.R.K. Ranger Park

https://www.nps.gov/pefo/planyourvisit/pets.htm

Redwood National and State Park (California, 1968)

Redwood is a unique park in the fact that it is a joint effort of both federal and state lands that protect the tallest trees on earth and the ecosystems they exist in. The park also encompasses 40 miles of rugged Northern California coastline. Redwood trees in this area can grow over 300 feet tall and around 2,000 years old. Wildlife is abundant in the area, from bears, deer, elk, cougars, and beavers to hundreds of species of birds. The park has over 200 miles of trails to explore.

Pets in Redwood:
There are specific areas within the parks where dogs are allowed. The following parking areas: Fern Canyon, Lady Bird Johnson, Tall Trees Trail, and Stout Grove parking lots only and Elk Meadow Day Use Area parking lot. The following overlooks: Klamath River Overlook and Redwood Creek Overlook. The following campgrounds: Elk Prairie, Gold Bluffs Beach, Mill Creek, and Jedediah Smith. The following beaches: Freshwater, Gold Bluffs, and Crescent. Cal Barrel Road in Prairie Creek Redwoods State Park and Walker Road in Jedediah Smith Redwoods State Park. Dogs are not allowed on any park trails or at ranger-led programs. Dogs must be on a leash no longer than 6 feet at all times, and pet waste must be picked up and placed in a trash receptacle.

B.A.R.K. Ranger Park

https://www.nps.gov/redw/planyourvisit/pets.htm

Saguaro National Park (Arizona, 1994)

Saguaro protects nearly two million of the saguaro cacti the park is named for due to concerns about the disappearing plants. The saguaro is a slow-growing cactus that lives approximately 150-175 years. They do not start growing branches to achieve the classic cactus silhouette until approximately 50 years old. The saguaros are only found in a small portion of the United States and are the nation's largest cacti, growing up to 40 feet tall. The park boasts beautiful sunsets that are iconic of Southwestern landscapes.

Pets in Saguaro:

Pets are allowed on roadways, picnic areas, and the paved Desert Ecology Trail and Desert Discovery Trail. Pets are allowed on the following trails and roads in the Eastern Rincon Mountain District: Mica View Dirt Road, Mica View Trail, Desert Ecology Trail, and the Cactus Forest Loop Road. Pets are allowed on the following trails and roads in the Western Tucson Mountain District: Bajada Loop Drive, Desert Discovery Trail, and Golden Gate Road. Pets are required to be on a leash at all times when they are outside of vehicles. Pets are not allowed on trails other than the ones listed above, off-road, or inside public buildings. Due to extreme temperatures, pets may not be left unattended in or outside a vehicle at any time.

https://www.nps.gov/sagu/planyourvisit/pets.htm

Shenandoah National Park (Virginia, 1935)

Shenandoah contains over 200,000 acres of protected land, including wooded hollows, fields of wildflowers, waterfalls, and abundant wildlife. The park has over 500 miles of hiking trails, including 105 miles of the Appalachian Trail. There is also considerable cultural history within the park. The peak season for Shenandoah is in September and October, when the temperatures start to drop, and the leaves start to change color. It is so popular that campgrounds and lodges are usually booked months in advance, and the park provides Fall color tracking via social media and webcams. On Thursdays, they provide a "Fall Broadcast" on Facebook and YouTube. A pass can be purchased online in advance to avoid long lines at the entrance gates. The park provides a special lane for those who already have an entrance pass.

Pets in Shenandoah:

Pets are allowed on roads, parking areas, campgrounds, and anywhere a public vehicle is allowed. Pets are also allowed on most park trails except the following: Fox Hollow, Stony Man (other than the portion that merges with the Appalachian Trail), Limberlost, Post Office Junction to Old Rag Shelter, Old Rag Ridge, Old Rag Saddle, Ridge Access (Old Rag area,) Dark Hollow Falls, Story of the Forest, Bearfence Mountain, Frazier Discovery. The prohibited trail list totals less than 20 miles of the over 500 miles of trails in the park, meaning there is abundant exploring that can be done with your pet. Per federal regulations, pets must be on a leash at all times when outside of a vehicle, no longer than 6 feet in length. Pet waste must be collected and deposited in trash receptacles. Pet waste must also be collected and packed out on trails, as pet waste can transfer illness and diseases to wildlife. Do not bag pet waste and leave it on the side of the trail, in trees, or on signposts. Pets are not allowed in park buildings or on Ranger-led programs.

https://www.nps.gov/shen/planyourvisit/pets.htm

Virgin Islands National Park (U.S. Virgin Islands, 1956)

Virgin Islands boasts beautiful white sand beaches and turquoise waters. The park is on St. John Island and covers two-thirds of the island. The park offers much more than just natural beauty and recreation opportunities, including around 3,000 years of human history. The earliest sign of visitors to the island is around 3,000 years ago, and the first known permanent inhabitants came to the island around 1,000 to 1,300 years ago with the Taino people. Taino culture can be explored at the Petroglyph site on Reef Bay Trail. It is unknown why the Taino people left the island, but Europeans next inhabited it from the early 1600s. They brought enslaved people from Africa and established a slave market in the port of Charlotte Amalie on St. Thomas. History shows a brutal period of enslavement until 1848, when slavery was abolished in the Danish West Indies. This period informs not only the past but also the current culture on the islands. Visit the parks, ruins, and plantations to explore more of this human history. The park also has opportunities for hiking, camping, and boating.

Pets in Virgin Islands:

Pets are allowed in the park and on trails. Pets must be on a leash no longer than 6 feet long, and pets can not be tied to an object and left unattended. Pet waste must be collected and placed in a trash receptacle. Pets are not allowed on beaches to protect nesting sea turtles and shore birds and for the enjoyment of other visitors. Pets are not allowed in park buildings.

https://www.nps.gov/viis/planyourvisit/pets.htm

Voyageurs National Park (Minnesota, 1975)

Voyageurs is a water-based park along the Canadian-American border. The park consists of over 218,000 acres, including islands surrounded by around 80,000 acres of lakes and waterways. There are only two primitive campsites in the park that do not require boat access. Around 200 campsites and houseboat sites within the park are accessible only by boat or houseboat. All campsites within the park require reservations and a permit. There are additional campgrounds outside the park. There are 27 miles of hiking trails. The park is also accessible during the winter with over 100 miles of groomed snowmobiling trails, snowshoe and cross-country skiing trails, ice fishing, and sledding opportunities. Voyageurs is also a certified Dark Sky Park.

Pets in Voyageurs:

Pets are allowed on roads, parking areas, and front country campsites. Pets are also allowed on the 1.7-mile Recreation Trail, which follows Country Road 96 from Highway 11 to Rainy Lake Visitor Center. Pets are required to be on a leash at all times, and pet waste must be promptly picked up and disposed of in trash receptacles. Pets are not allowed at the backcountry sites located within the Kabetogama Peninsula or on tour boats.

https://www.nps.gov/voya/planyourvisit/pets.htm

White Sands National Park (New Mexico, 2019)

White Sands protects the largest gypsum dune field on the planet, 275 square miles of white wave-like dunes of gypsum sand in the Tularosa Basin. The sand was left behind when a lake that used to fill the basin evaporated thousands of years ago. Only 115 of the 275 square miles are protected by the park, with the remainder on a military installation outside the park. The park is occasionally closed due to missile testing, so checking for closures before planning a visit is best. The park was designated as a National Monument in 1933 and just recently added to the National Park System in 2019.

Pets in White Sands:

Pets are welcome in all areas of White Sands except for the visitor center. White Sands is very pet friendly, and to ensure that it stays that way, make sure to keep your pets leashed at all times outside of vehicles and clean up after your pets.

There are two pet waste stations near the Visitor Center for your convenience. Please keep in mind that many people enjoy walking barefoot in the sand, as well as playing and sledding, and picking up your pet's waste is not only required but also considerate of the enjoyment of other guests. Temperatures can reach extremes in vehicles and pets should not be left in vehicles for their safety. It is prohibited to leave pets unattended and tied to an object.

https://www.nps.gov/whsa/planyourvisit/pets.htm

Wind Cave National Park (South Dakota, 1903)

Wind Cave is one of the few national parks that exists, and can be visited, both above and below the earth's surface. Wind Cave is one of the longest and most complex caves in the world. There are a few different guided tour options to explore the caves. Above the caves, wildlife roams the prairies like they have for centuries, including bison and elk. Wind Cave was one of the earliest national parks as the 6th area designated as a National Park in the United States. Also of interest in the area is the National Monument, Mount Rushmore, located near Wind Cave, and the independent and non-profit Crazy Horse Memorial.

Pets in Wind Cave:
Pets are allowed in the Elk Mountain Campground, the grassy areas near the visitor center, public roads, and parking areas. Pets are also allowed on the Prairie Vista Trail and Elk Mountain Campground Trail. Pets are always required to be on a leash

outside a vehicle, and pet waste must be picked up and properly disposed of in trash receptacles. Pets are not permitted in the park's backcountry areas, on any trails not listed above, or in public buildings. Pets are not allowed on ranger-led programs or in the caves.

https://www.nps.gov/wica/planyourvisit/pets.htm

Wrangell-St. Elias National Park & Preserve (Alaska, 1980)

Wrangell-St. Elias is America's largest national park. It contains 13.2 million acres, which is equivalent to the size of six Yellowstone National Parks. In addition to the large acreage, it rises from sea level to 18,008ft. Mount St. Elias is the second-highest peak in both the U.S. and Canada. The park contains some of the largest volcanoes and the greatest concentration of glaciers in North America, with around 30 percent of the park covered in glaciers. The park also preserves a subsistence lifestyle for Alaska natives and rural Alaska residents who rely on the land.

Pets in Wrangell-St. Elias

Unlike most national parks, dogs are allowed on trails and in the backcountry of Wrangell-St. Elias. Per N.P.S. (National Park Service) regulations, all pets should be on a leash no longer than 6 feet. This policy is for your and your pet's safety and protecting and preserving the land, ecosystem, and wildlife. Trapping is allowed within the park boundaries during specific seasons and can also pose a risk to loose pets.

*B.A.R.K. Ranger Park

https://www.nps.gov/wrst/planyourvisit/pets.htm

Zion National Park (Utah, 1919)

Zion was the first of the current five national parks in Utah. Morman pioneers named the area Zion, meaning "promise land." The park features unique opportunities to hike in slot canyons, The Narrows, or the steep trek up to Angel's Landing. The park has around a dozen miles of paved trails and over 100 miles of wilderness trails in addition to canyoneering routes. The park can be very busy during the peak summer season, and advanced planning is advised.

Pets in Zion:

Pets are allowed on and along public roads and parking areas, drive-in campgrounds, picnic areas, and on the grounds of Zion Lodge. Pets are allowed on the Pa'rus Trail, which begins at the Zion Canyon Visitor Center. Pets are not permitted on any other trails, in the backcountry wilderness areas, on shuttle buses, or in public buildings. It gets hot in Zion, and pets should not be left in vehicles, even with cracked windows. Properly restrained pets may be left unattended in developed campgrounds only when environmental conditions are safe for the animal. If a pet is at risk of making an unreasonable amount of noise, such as barking, they should not be left unattended.

https://www.nps.gov/zion/planyourvisit/pets.htm

6

The Dog-Friendly National Parks

In this chapter, you will be introduced to the National Parks, which have the most commonly restricted access for pets. Parks are listed in alphabetical order, not in order of most access, to make finding the park you are interested in quicker and easier. Following the park name in parenthesis are the state(s) in which the park is located, and the year it was established as a National Park.

While it is our intention to provide the most accurate and up-to-date information at the time of writing and publication, it is always advised to visit the website (links are provided) or inquire at the visitor center regarding pet access. Doing this will ensure that you have the most up-to-date information on closed trails, seasonally protected areas, and other closures, and will also provide notification of any potential health risks that may affect your pet. This book is meant to be a quick and easy offline guide and supplement to aid in preparation and planning enjoyable visits to the National Parks, but it cannot guarantee that the information, access, and restrictions may not change after publication.

The parks in this section only allow dogs in campgrounds, picnic areas, on park roads, or in parking lots.

Arches National Park (Utah, 1971)

Arches is named after the over 2,000 natural stone arches, up to 112 feet high. In addition to the arches, there are hundreds of pinnacles, massive rock fins, and giant balanced rocks in the land of red rock. The sky is just as beautiful as the land here, with incredible sunsets and low light pollution for ideal night sky viewing. Arches was designated a National Monument in 1929 and became a National Park in 1971.

Pets in Arches:
   Pets are allowed along established roads and in parking areas. They are also allowed in drive-in campgrounds and established picnic areas. Pets are not allowed on any hiking trails, off trail, in any public buildings, or overlooks. Pets must be on a leash but may not be led on a leash by bicycle or from a vehicle. Pets that are held or in carriers of any sort must adhere to the restrictions of leashed pets. Pets may not be left unattended in vehicles if it creates a danger to the animal or if the animal becomes a nuisance.

https://www.nps.gov/arch/planyourvisit/pets.htm

Badlands National Park (South Dakota, 1978)

Badlands protects not only an interesting landscape but a landscape that contains one of the world's richest known fossil beds, letting us know that ancient horses and rhinos once roamed on this land. Today, you will not see rhinos, but you can see bison, bighorn sheep, prairie dogs, and black-footed ferrets. The Lakota people called the area mako sica for hundreds of years, which translates to "bad lands." French fur trappers called the area les mauvaises terres a traveser ('bad lands to travel across'). Why "bad lands?" The landscape posed many challenges to traveling through the area. The summers are hot, the winters are cold and windy, and evidence of early activity points to more season hunting than settlements and habitation. The area was first proposed as a national park in 1922 with a name change, but the historical name was kept when it was finally designated as a national park in 1978.

Pets in Badlands:

Pets are allowed in developed areas where vehicles are allowed, such as campgrounds, picnic areas, gravel or paved roadways, roadway corridors, and parking lots. Pets are required to be on a leash at all times outside of vehicles. It is required to pick up after your pets and deposit waste into trash receptacles. Pets are not allowed on hiking trails, in public buildings, backcountry areas, including the Badlands Wilderness Area, or areas with prairie dog colonies.

https://www.nps.gov/badl/planyourvisit/basicinfo.htm

Big Bend National Park (Texas, 1944)

Big Bend was recognized as a special place by the state of Texas in the early 1930s and joined the National Park System in 1944. The beauty of the canyons in the Big Bend of the Rio Grande River was what initially caught the attention of those with conservation in mind. The landscape is not all that Big Bend has to offer. The park is also rich in sea fossils and dinosaur bones. It is also home to a wide diversity of species. The park is located in the far west part of Texas along the Rio Grande River and the Mexican border. Because of this location, the park also has a long, diverse human history. Also, due to the location, the best time to visit the park is from late Fall through early Spring, as the summer temperatures during the days get extremely high.

Pets in Big Bend:

Pets are allowed in areas where public vehicles are allowed, such as public roadways and parking lots. Pets must be on a leash at all times when outside of vehicles, and pet waste must be promptly picked up and placed in an appropriate trash receptacle. Pets are not allowed on trails, off of roads, or on the river. Pets are not allowed to go into Mexico at the Boquillas Port of Entry. Pets are not permitted to be left in vehicles if it creates a danger to the animal or if the animal becomes a public nuisance.

https://www.nps.gov/bibe/planyourvisit/pets.htm

Canyonlands National Park (Utah, 1964)

Canyonlands is split into three land districts: Island in the Sky, Needles, and Maze. The confluence of the Green River and Colorado River defines the three districts. Island in the Sky is so named for the broad mesa that has a view 2,000 feet of the river below. Needles features red and white banded pinnacles and arches. And the least visited of the three, the Maze, is home to ancient rock art panels and a labyrinth of canyons called the Doll House. In addition to the three land districts, the rivers are considered a fourth district within the park.

Pets in Canyonlands:

Pets are allowed along established roads and in parking areas. They are also allowed in drive-in campgrounds and established picnic areas. Pets may be transported inside vehicles driving the Shafer Trail to Potash Road at Island in the Sky. When the road to Beef Basin via Cathedral Butte is closed by snow or mud, persons with pets are allowed to cross the Needles district via the Elephant Hill-Devil's Lane/Bobby's Hole roads. Pets are not allowed on any hiking trails, off trail, in the backcountry, in public buildings, or at overlooks. Pets are not allowed on river trips. Pets that are held or in carriers of any sort must adhere to the restrictions of leashed pets. Pets may not be tied to any object other than your personal vehicle. Pets may not be left unattended overnight, tied up where it would interfere with wildlife or travel by others, or in a way that natural resources would be damaged.

https://www.nps.gov/cany/planyourvisit/pets.htm

Carlsbad Caverns National Park (New Mexico, 1930)

Carlsbad Caverns is one of the cave system parks that exists, and can be explored, both above and below the earth's surface. The park contains around 119 caves that were formed when sulfuric acid dissolved the limestone rock. Above the caves, on the surface of the Chihuahuan Desert, the landscape features ancient sea ledges, deep rocky canyons, as well as desert plants and wildlife. The cave can be explored through ranger-guided tours as well as on your own; however, timed entry tickets are required for entry. The park also has a Bat Flight Program that runs from late May through October. The free ranger talk occurs nightly before Brazilian free-tailed bats emerge from the cavern to hunt for food. The bats migrate for the winter and usually return to the caverns in mid-to-late April. The park also has Night Sky Programs and night hikes after the Bat Flight Program.

Pets in Carlsbad Caverns:
    Pets are allowed on paved roads and in parking lots. Pets must be on a leash at all times when outside of a vehicle. Always clean up after your pet and place waste in trash receptacles. Pets are prohibited in the caverns, on unpaved park trails, off-road, during the Bat Flight Program, or in the Visitor Center. Pets are not allowed to be left unattended in vehicles. They must be kenneled. Carlsbad Caverns Trading Company operates a day kennel in the park. Please see the website for hours and requirements.

https://www.nps.gov/cave/planyourvisit/pets.htm

Death Valley National Park (California & Nevada, 1994)

Death Valley is where the lowest point in North America, at 282 feet below sea level, can be found at Badwater Basin. The basin is what is left of a prehistoric lake. The park is also known for the highest temperature ever recorded when the temperature reached 134 degrees in July of 1913. The salt flats in the park are also among the largest in the world. Despite its name, there are over 400 species of animals in the park. While known for its desert landscape and high summer temperatures, snow covers the peaks in the park during the winters. Wildflowers can be seen in the park in the Spring. The park was designated as a national monument in 1933, prior to becoming a national park. The landscape has gone through drastic changes over the years, and the park also has a rich cultural history.

Pets in Death Valley:

Pets are allowed on leash in established areas such as roads, drive-in campgrounds, parking lots, and picnic areas. Pets are essentially allowed anywhere a car can go in the park. They are allowed on both paved and dirt roads, including the following: 20 Mule Team Canyon, Devil's Golf Course Road, Father Crowley Point spur road to Padre Point, Furnace Creek Airport Road, Lake Hill Road, Mustard Canyon Road, Titus Canyon Road, and Cottonwood-Marble Access Road. Pets are not allowed on dirt or paved trails, boardwalks, in the wilderness, in park buildings, or in historic structures. Pets in carriers and backpacks are allowed only where leashed pets are allowed. Do not leave pets unattended or out of sight at campsites. Pets have attracted predatory animals while tethered at campsites or resting under campers or vehicles. Do not leave food and water outside unattended; this can attract wildlife. It is not advised to bring pets to Death Valley from late Spring through early Fall due to high temperatures.

https://www.nps.gov/deva/planyourvisit/pets.htm

Everglades National Park (Florida, 1934)

Everglades protects 1.5 million acres, containing the largest subtropical wilderness in the United States. This area is an essential habitat for rare and endangered species such as the Florida panther, the manatee, and the American crocodile. The park is also protected under the Cartagena Treaty, is a World Heritage Site, an International Biosphere Reserve, and a Wetland of International Importance. Recreation in the park includes bicycling, boating, camping, kayaking and canoeing, fishing, hiking and slough slogging, guided tours, and ranger-led programs. The park has two seasons: wet season and dry season. The wet season is typically from May to November, and the dry season is typically from December through April. The dry season is a more desirable time to visit the park due to high temperatures, rainfall, and mosquito activity during the wet season and because it is a better time for viewing wildlife.

Pets in Everglades:
   Pets are allowed on public roadways open to vehicular traffic, drive-in campgrounds, picnic areas, and parking lots. Pets are also allowed on maintained grounds surrounding public facilities, residential areas, and in private boats. Pets are not

permitted on any trails, paved or unpaved, including Shark Valley Tram Trail/Road. Pets are not permitted on unpaved roads. Pets must be on a leash at all times, no longer than 6 feet in length. Pets must not be left unattended or tethered outside unattended. Pet waste must be collected and deposited into a trash receptacle.

https://www.nps.gov/ever/planyourvisit/pets.htm

Glacier National Park (Montana, 1910)

Glacier is known as the Crown of the Continent and was named Glacier National Park for its 150 glaciers that were counted in 1850. Now, only around 25 glaciers are left in the park. In addition to the glaciers, the park has hundreds of beautiful lakes, mountain landscapes, 700 miles of hiking trails, and abundant wildlife, including Rocky Mountain bighorn sheep and mountain goats. The park is located in northwestern Montana along the Canadian border. Due to its short season, beautiful scenery, road construction, and road conditions, visiting this park is best done with advanced planning.

Pets in Glacier:
  Pets are allowed in developed areas such as drive-in camp-grounds, picnic areas, along roads, in parking areas, and in boats on lakes where motorized watercraft are permitted. When free of snow, dogs are allowed on leash on the bike path between Apgar and West Glacier. Pets are not allowed on trails, in the backcountry, buildings, or along lake shores outside developed

locations. Pets can not ride loose in the back of a pickup; they must be in a crate or under physical restraint. Pets are not to be left tied to an object unattended. Please note: when roads are closed to vehicle traffic, they are considered a backcountry trail, and pets are prohibited.

https://www.nps.gov/glac/planyourvisit/pets.htm

Grand Teton National Park (Wyoming, 1929)

Grand Teton is known for its iconic Teton mountain range and is located south of Yellowstone National Park. Alpine landscapes and wildlife are great viewing in the park. There are over 200 miles of hiking trails and recreational opportunities for rock climbing and boating on the Snake River and the park lakes.

Pets in Grand Teton:
  Pets are allowed on any roads vehicles are allowed, in turnouts, picnic areas, and in developed drive-in campgrounds. They must be within 30 feet of any roadway. In the winter, pets may walk in the designated pet walking lane on the closed portions of Teton Park Road, but pets are prohibited from destroying the groomed cross-country ski track. Pets are not allowed in the backcountry, on trails, on beaches, or on the park's multi-use pathway. Pets are prohibited from swimming in park waters and in park buildings. Pets are prohibited from riding in boats on park waters, with the exception of Jackson Lake.

https://www.nps.gov/grte/planyourvisit/pets.htm

Haleakalā National Park (Hawai'i, 1961)

Haleakalā features a rocky coastline, lush rainforests, and scenic views. Sunsets are so popular in the Summit District they require a permit. The Haleakalā volcano formed most of the island of Maui. The volcano is also significant and sacred in Polynesian culture. In addition to the beautiful scenery, the park also protects more endangered species than any other national park. There are 103 endangered species, including plants, birds, insects, mammals, and a single reptile.

Pets in Haleakalā:
   Dogs are permitted in parking lots and drive-up campgrounds, roadways, and paved pathways only. Dogs must be on a leash at all times. Dogs are not permitted on trails or at remote campsites or wilderness cabins.

https://www.nps.gov/hale/planyourvisit/pets.htm

Hawai'i Volcanoes National Park (Hawai'i, 1916)

Hawai'i Volcanoes is home to two of the world's most active volcanoes, Mauna Loa and Kīlauea. Mauna Loa is the largest active volcano on Earth, but Kīlauea is the most productive. Like Haleakalā National Park, Hawai'i Volcanoes is home to a large number of endangered species. Hawai'i Volcanoes is a designated International Biosphere Reserve and UNESCO World Heritage Site. The park can be explored by driving the road tours, such as Crater Rim Drive Tour or the Chain of Craters Road Tour.

There are also day hikes and backcountry hiking opportunities as well. Always check with the visitor center or backcountry office for current conditions and backcountry requirements.

Pets in Hawai'i Volcanoes:

Hawai'i Volcanoes has specific areas where pets are allowed and not allowed. Pets are allowed in the following areas: All parking areas (excluding Hilina Pali Road and Kulanaokuaiki Campground), on Crater Rim Drive in areas open to vehicles, on Chain of Craters Road down to Pu'uloa Petroglyphs, Nāmaka-nipaio Campground, Mauna Loa Road (occasionally referred to as "The Strip Road"), on Highway 11, and at Kīlauea Military Camp (on paved roads and parking areas; and at the picnic area, up to the park ball field gate, not including the ball field.) Pets are allowed in the following areas of the Kahuku Unit: Developed areas that include the open fields adjacent to the Visitor Contact Station and the area that extends to the boundary of the forested areas up to, but not including Pu'u o Lokuana, Kahuku Road from Highway 11 to the cross fence gate, including the airstrip by the intersection of Pu'u o Lokuana, and Old Mamalahoa Highway spur road. Pets are not allowed in the following areas: all undeveloped areas of the park, including all designated wilderness and all front-country and backcountry trails, and park buildings.

B.A.R.K. Ranger Park

https://www.nps.gov/havo/planyourvisit/pets.htm

Joshua Tree National Park (California, 1994)

Joshua Tree is named after the unique Joshua trees, which are part of the Agave family. These trees grow up to forty feet tall and are estimated to be up to 150 years old. In addition to the Joshua Trees, the granite boulders define the unique landscape. High temperatures in the summer and chilly to freezing temperatures in the winter are part of this desert climate. The Mojave and the Colorado deserts meet in Joshua Tree National Park.

Pets in Joshua Tree:

Pets are allowed on leash in drive-in campgrounds, parking lots, and picnic areas. Pets are essentially allowed anywhere a vehicle can go. Please note that some unpaved roads require 4-wheel drive. Pets are also permitted on the paved Oasis of Mara and Keys View trails. Climbing areas accessible with a dog include Belle Campground (Castle Rock), Hidden Valley Campground (Many but not all of the climbs are within 100 ft of a road, parking area, or campsite), Indian Cove Area (Billboard Buttress, King Otto's Castle, Pixie Rock, and Short Wall), Quail Springs Area (Trash Can.) Paved trails, roads, and parking areas can get hot in the summer and should be taken into consideration for the safety and comfort of your pet. Pets are not allowed in the backcountry, on trails other than the two listed above, or in park buildings. Pet waste must be collected and disposed of in a trash receptacle or dumpster. It is prohibited to leave a pet unattended or tied to an object. Due to high temperatures, it can be lethal to leave pets in vehicles even with windows slightly open.

https://www.nps.gov/jotr/planyourvisit/pets.htm

Kenai Fjords National Park (Alaska, 1980)

Kenai Fjords is home to the Harding Icefield, one of only four ice fields left in the United States. Exit Glacier is the only feature of the park that is accessible by road, with the majority of the park viewed by boat. The fjords reaching from the Gulf of Alaska into the southern part of the park are a haven for wildlife. Boaters can spot sea otters, seals, porpoises, orcas, whales, and numerous species of birds. Along the shoreline, it is possible to see moose, grizzly bears, and black bears.

Pets in Kenai Fjords:
    Pets are allowed on the road to Exit Glacier, the Herman Leirer Road, and in the parking lot of the Exit Glacier Nature Center. Dogs are not allowed on any trails, including the trails in the Exit Glacier area or the Harding Icefield Trail. Pets are not allowed in the coastal backcountry. Pets are not allowed along the coast in an area extending from the mean high tide line to a quarter of a mile inland from May 30th through November 1st.

https://www.nps.gov/kefj/planyourvisit/pets.htm

Lassen Volcanic National Park (California, 1916)

Lassen Volcanic is the only national park to encompass all four types of volcanos: plug dome, composite, cinder cone, and shield. Water from snowmelt and rain seeps into the ground, where it is heated by molten rock below the surface. This heated water creates the hydrothermal features such as hot springs, fumaroles, and boiling mud pots that can be found in the park. Lassen Peak last erupted in 1914 and spewed lava for several years. It is still one of the biggest plug dome volcanoes in the world. The park has around 150 miles of hiking trails to explore the wild landscape.

Pets in Lassen Volcanic:
   Pets are allowed anywhere you can go with your vehicle; this means roads, road shoulders (when not snow-covered,) drive-in campgrounds, picnic areas, and parking lots. Dogs must always be on a leash no longer than 6 feet long. Pets are not permitted on any hiking trails, in the backcountry (including snow-covered roads or trails), in any body of water, or inside visitor centers or other park facilities.

https://www.nps.gov/lavo/planyourvisit/pets.htm

Mount Rainier National Park (Washington, 1899)

Mount Rainier, an active volcano, reaches 14,410 feet above sea level and is the most glaciated peak in the contiguous U.S. In addition to this notable peak, the park boasts beautiful landscapes, mountain and valley lake views, and lovely wildflowers. An abundance of hiking opportunities exist within the park.

Pets in Mount Rainier:

Pets are allowed on paved roads and within 6 feet from the edge of the road, in parking lots, and in drive-in campgrounds. Pets are allowed on the Longmire Historic District Walking Tour. Dogs are also allowed on the Pacific Crest Trail (PCT). Please note: a portion of the PCT is used to form the Naches Peak Loop Trail near Tipsoo Lake, and while dogs are allowed on the PCT portion, they are not allowed on the non-PCT sections of the loop within the park. Dogs are prohibited on all trails and in the park's wilderness areas. Carbon River Road and Westside Road are closed to vehicles and pets. Dogs must be on leash at all times within the park.

https://www.nps.gov/mora/planyourvisit/pets.htm

North Cascades National Park (Washington, 1968)

North Cascades is named after the cascading waterfalls in this mountainous park. The park has more than 300 glaciers, hundreds of alpine lakes, and abundant wildlife. There are only 6 miles of unpaved roads in the park but over 400 miles of hiking trails. From day hikes to overnight backcountry hikes and boating, there are many ways to explore the park.

Pets in North Cascades:

In addition to the roads open to vehicle travel, parking lots, and drive-in campgrounds, pets are allowed within the Ross Lake and Lake Chelan National Recreation Areas. (These are part of the North Cascades National Park Service Complex but are of the National Park Boundaries.) Dogs are also allowed on the Pacific Crest Trail. Dogs are not permitted on trails, in the backcountry, or in park buildings. Dogs must be on leash at all times within the park.

https://www.nps.gov/noca/planyourvisit/pets.htm

Pinnacles National Park (California, 2013)

Pinnacles only recently became a national park, but the creation of the landscape that we know today began around 23 million years ago as volcanoes erupted and flowed. Over many years, the features created by these volcanoes moved nearly 200 miles along the San Andreas Fault with the help of earthquakes and other tectonic forces. The park was declared a national monument in 1908 to protect the land that has become a national park. In addition to the unique landscape, the park has been instrumental in helping to bring the California condors back from the brink of extinction.

Pets in Pinnacles:
   Pets are allowed on paved roads, in parking lots, drive-in campgrounds, and picnic areas. Pets must be on a leash at a length no longer than 6 feet. Pet waste must be cleaned up, regardless of where you are, and disposed of in appropriate trash receptacles or dumpsters. Please note temperatures in

the summer can hit triple digits and higher inside vehicles.

https://www.nps.gov/pinn/planyourvisit/pets.htm

Rocky Mountain National Park (Colorado, 1915)

Rocky Mountain is one of the most visited parks due to its close proximity to Denver. Situated in the Colorado Rockies, the park boasts majestic mountain views. Trail Ridge Road in the park climbs to 12,183 feet to the Continental Divide and is the highest continuously paved road in the United States. The park is also home to a wide range of wildlife. In addition to over 300 miles of hiking trails, the park is also a rock climbing destination.

Pets in Rocky Mountain:
   Pets are allowed on paved roads, in parking lots, drive-in campgrounds, and picnic areas. Pets must be on a leash at a length no longer than 6 feet. Pet waste must be cleaned up, regardless of where you are, and disposed of in appropriate trash receptacles or dumpsters. Dogs are not allowed in backcountry wilderness areas, in meadows, on trails, on tundra, or in park buildings. Pets may not be left tied to vehicles, trees, or other objects and may not be unattended if it is a danger to the pet or the pet would be considered a nuisance.

https://www.nps.gov/romo/planyourvisit/pets.htm

Sequoia & Kings Canyon National Parks (California, 1890 & 1940)

Sequoia and Kings Canyon are joint parks in the Sierra Nevada mountain range. John Muir attempted to establish both parks but only succeeded in securing Sequoia's place in the national park system at that time. It wasn't until 1940 that King's Canyon joined Sequoia in the national park ranks. The joint parks encompass one of the deepest canyons in North America, Kings Canyon, and the highest point in the contiguous United States, Mount Whitney, as well as the largest tree by volume, General Sherman. There are around 8,000 sequoias in the Giant Forest. In addition to many of these trees being 2000-3000 years old and some of the largest trees on earth, they are fascinating in their evolution with fire. The trees have thick, fire-resistant bark that protects and insulates the trees during wildfires. And their seeds actually need fire. Fire helps release the seeds from cones, and the seeds require bare soil cleared by fire to germinate. The fires also create rich soil that helps these seeds get off to a good start.

Pets in Sequoia & Kings Canyon:

Pets are only allowed outside a vehicle and on leash in the following locations: paved roads, parking lots, drive-in campgrounds, and picnic areas. Pets are not allowed in wilderness areas or on any trails, including paved trails such as the General Sherman Tree Trail, Big Trees Trail, Grant Tree Trail, and others. Pets are allowed in carriers and backpacks but are only allowed where leashed pets are allowed. Pet waste must be picked up and properly disposed of in appropriate trash receptacles. Pet food must be properly stored to avoid attracting bears, including in picnic areas and campgrounds. Pets may not be left tethered and unattended.

https://www.nps.gov/seki/planyourvisit/pets.htm

Theodore Roosevelt National Park (North Dakota, 1978)

Theodore Roosevelt is named after the 26th President of the United States. Not only was Theodore (Teddy) Roosevelt the youngest person to become president at age 42 and the first American to ever win a Nobel Prize when he won the Nobel Peace Prize in 1906, he also played a large role in conservation efforts that led to the formation of the first protected lands and national parks. Roosevelt first went to North Dakota, known then as the Dakota Territory, to hunt bison in 1883. He would later purchase a cattle ranch that sits along the Little Missouri River and between what is now the North and South sections of Theodore Roosevelt Park. Roosevelt's Elkhorn Ranch is also a unit of the park and can be visited when visiting the park. Visiting the ranch entails driving on unpaved roads that may require a 4-wheel drive and high clearance vehicle, depending on weather and road conditions. Enjoy the park with scenic drives, hiking, and wildlife viewing.

Pets in Theodore Roosevelt:
Pets are allowed along roads and on shoulders, on sidewalks, in parking areas, and in campgrounds and picnic areas. The best places to walk your pet on hot days are the campgrounds and picnic areas where there is shade. Pets must be on a leash at all

times when outside of vehicles. Pets are not allowed on trails or in park buildings.

https://www.nps.gov/thro/planyourvisit/pets.htm

Yellowstone National Park (Wyoming, Montana, & Idaho, 1872)

Yellowstone was the first area in the United States to be designated as a national park. That is just one of the things that makes this park special, however. The park sits on one of the earth's largest supervolcanoes, which created the unique landscape and is responsible for the unique hydrothermal and geologic features such as geysers, fumaroles, mud pots, hot springs, and vents. Yellowstone contains about half of the world's active geysers, with the most well-known geyser being Old Faithful. Bison in the Yellowstone region are the most genetically pure herds in North America, and it is the only place in the United States where they have lived continuously since prehistoric times. Bison are the largest land-dwelling mammal in North America and can run up to 35mph. In addition to bison, Yellowstone is home to the largest concentration of mammals in the lower 48 states, including grizzly bears, elk, wolves, moose, and mountain lions.

Pets in Yellowstone:
 Pets are allowed in developed areas where vehicles are allowed and must remain within 100 feet of roads, parking areas, and drive-in campgrounds. Pets must be physically controlled at all times in a car, in a crate, or on a leash no longer than 6ft long. Pets are not allowed on boardwalks, hiking trails, near wildlife,

in park buildings, in the backcountry, or in thermal areas. Please note: there are no exceptions to the restricted areas for carried pets, including in carriers, strollers, backpacks, etc.

https://www.nps.gov/yell/planyourvisit/pets.htm

Yosemite National Park (California, 1890)

Yosemite is best known for its waterfalls and rock climbing. What you may not know is that Yosemite Falls is North America's tallest waterfall, El Capitan is the world's tallest granite monolith, Half Dome's sheer cliff is the largest in North America, and the sequoia trees are some of the oldest living things on earth. These are just a few things that bring over four million visitors to the park each year, from rock climbers to families. The park is open year-round, but Spring is when waterfall viewing is at its peak with early snowmelt.

Pets in Yosemite:

Pets are allowed in developed areas such as paved roads, sidewalks, and bicycle paths unless otherwise marked. Pets are also allowed in call drive-in campgrounds. Pets are allowed on the Wawona Meadow Loop but are not allowed on any other trails, including the trail to Vernal Fall. Pets are not allowed in undeveloped or wilderness areas, walk-in or group campgrounds, on unplowed roads covered in snow, on shuttle buses, in lodging areas or public buildings, or any other posted areas. Please note: there are no exceptions to the restricted areas for carried pets, including in carriers, strollers, backpacks,

74

etc.

B.A.R.K. Ranger Park

https://www.nps.gov/yose/planyourvisit/pets.htm

7

The Least Dog-Friendly National Parks

In this chapter, you will be introduced to the National Parks, which have the least access for pets. Parks are listed in alphabetical order, not in order of most access, to make finding the park you are interested in quicker and easier. Following the park name in parenthesis are the state(s) in which the park is located, and the year it was established as a National Park.

While it is our intention to provide the most accurate and up-to-date information at the time of writing and publication, it is always advised to visit the website (links are provided) or inquire at the visitor center regarding pet access. Doing this will not only ensure that you have the most up-to-date information on closed trails, seasonally protected areas, and other closures, but it will also provide notification of any potential health risks that may affect your pet. This book is meant to be a quick and easy offline guide and supplement to aid in preparation and planning enjoyable visits to the National Parks, but it cannot guarantee that the information, access, and restrictions may not change after publication.

The national parks in this section are the parks that have the most restrictions on pets.

Glacier Bay National Park & Preserve (Alaska, 1980)

Glacier Bay encompasses over one thousand glaciers, including seven tidewater glaciers. It has over 3 million acres of mountains, temperate rainforests, wilderness, wildlife, and cultural legacy. The park is part of a 25 million-acre World Heritage Site, which is one of the world's largest international protected areas.

Pets in Glacier Bay:

Pets are allowed in Glacier Bay on the Bartlett Cove Public Use Dock and within 100 feet of Bartlett Cove Developed Area park roads or parking areas unless otherwise posted. Pets are also allowed on a private vessel on the water. While pets are allowed in limited areas, the park recommends leaving pets at home due to the park being a sanctuary for Alaskan wildlife. Pets are not allowed on trails, beaches, or in the backcountry.

https://www.nps.gov/glba/planyourvisit/pets.htm

Lake Clark National Park & Preserve (Alaska, 1980)

Lake Clark National Park & Preserve has mountains, volcanoes, glaciers, turquoise lakes, and abundant wildlife. It contains the largest sockeye salmon fishery in the world. It also preserves the land and culture of the Dena'ina people.

Pets in Lake Clark:

While dogs are permitted in the park with the standard restrictions, the park strongly urges that pets be left at home for their safety and the health and preservation of the ecosystem. Bringing dogs into the ecosystem could disrupt, disturb, or even kill wildlife as well as contract or spread disease. Because there are no roads to or in the park, and access to the park requires a plane or boat, bringing pets can also be difficult and expensive.

https://www.nps.gov/lacl/planyourvisit/pets.htm

National Park of the American Samoa (American Samoa, 1988)

American Samoa is a park in the South Pacific that provides an experience unlike any other national park. In addition to the beaches and the only mixed-species paleotropical rainforest in the United States, the park protects what is called "fa'asamoa," which is the customs, beliefs, and traditions of the 3,000-year-old Samoan culture. The Samoan culture is the oldest Polynesian culture. The park includes sections of three volcanic islands and 4,000 acres off their shores. It is the most remote national park in the system.

Pets in American Samoa:

Pets are not explicitly prohibited in the park; however, the park website states that pets, especially dogs, pose a threat to hikers and other park visitors and to park resources. Pets are not allowed in public buildings, on public transportation vehicles, on swimming beaches, or in structures. Pets are not allowed on hiking trails.

https://www.nps.gov/npsa/planyourvisit/pets.htm

8

National Parks With No Access for Pets

In this chapter, you will be introduced to the National Parks, which have no pet access. Parks are listed in alphabetical order, not in order of most access, to make finding the park you are interested in quicker and easier. Following the park name in parenthesis are the state(s) in which the park is located, and the year it was established as a National Park.

While it is our intention to provide the most accurate and up-to-date information at the time of writing and publication, it is always advised to visit the website (links are provided) or inquire at the visitor center regarding pet access. Doing this will not only ensure that you have the most up-to-date information on closed trails, seasonally protected areas, and other closures, but it will also provide notification of any potential health risks that may affect your pet. This book is meant to be a quick and easy offline guide and supplement to aid in preparation and planning enjoyable visits to the National Parks, but it cannot guarantee that the information, access, and restrictions may not change after publication.

The parks in this section do not allow dogs or strongly advise against bringing them into the park.

Channel Islands National Park (California, 1980)

Channel Islands encompasses five of the eight Channel Islands: San Miguel, Santa Rosa, Santa Cruz, Anacapa, and Santa Barbara. Over 2000 species of plants and animals live on the islands, and because of thousands of years of isolation in the Pacific Ocean, 145 of those species only exist on these islands and nowhere else on Earth. The oldest human remains found in North America were found on Santa Rosa Island and dated back to more than 13,000 years ago. The park is located twenty miles off California's coast and accessible only by boat or plane. Hiking, backpacking, camping, snorkeling, scuba diving, and kayaking are all activities available at the park. In addition to everything the park offers, traveling to and from the islands may also provide whale watching and dolphin sightings.

Pets on Channel Islands:
  Pets are not allowed on any of the Channel Islands. Not only does travel to the islands inhibit taking pets, but pets can bring parasites and diseases that could be devastating to the isolated animals living on the islands.

https://www.nps.gov/chis/planyourvisit/pets.htm

Isle Royale National Park (Michigan, 1940)

Isle Royale is an island in Lake Superior of the Great Lakes and is accessed by boat or seaplane from Michigan or Minnesota. Activities in the park include hiking, backpacking, paddling, and diving. Ten major shipwrecks within the park waters can be explored by experienced divers. Isle Royale is one of the parks that require more planning in advance to acquire camping permits if a stay on the island is part of the itinerary and to access the park by booking a boat or seaplane trip.

Pets in Isle Royale:

Pets are not permitted on the island. Pets are also prohibited from being on boats within the park boundaries, which extends 4 1/2 miles into Lake Superior from the outermost land areas of the park. Leashed pets are allowed outdoors at the Houghton Visitor Center and Headquarters complex where the Ranger III departs. Pets should not be left unattended in vehicles when temperatures create hazardous conditions.

https://www.nps.gov/isro/planyourvisit/pets.htm

Katmai National Park & Preserve (Alaska, 1980)

Katmai National Park was established as a national monument in 1918 after the largest volcanic eruption of the 20th century occurred and altered the landscape. Since then, it has become home to one of the largest populations of brown bears. Katmai became a National Park in 1980 and is currently the 4th largest national park in the United States. The park also helps preserve the cultural history of the people who have lived on the land for the past 9,000 years. There are no roads going to the park or within the park. Most visitors access the park by plane or boat.

Pets in Katmai:
   While Katmai National Park does not explicitly state that they allow or restrict dog or pet access, logistics to get to the park make bringing a pet difficult, expensive, and inconvenient.

https://www.nps.gov/katm

Kobuk Valley National Park (Alaska, 1980)

Kobuk Valley National Park is known for sand dunes, which can reach over 100ft tall, the Kobuk River, and the thousands of caribou that migrate through the park each year. Kobuk Valley is one of the most remote national parks, located North of the Arctic Circle. It does not have roads, entrance gates, or campgrounds. Access to the park requires flying on a series of airplanes and then backpacking, boating, or seeing the park by plane.

Pets in Kobuk Valley:
   While Kobuk Valley National Park does not explicitly state that they allow or restrict dog or pet access, logistics to the park make bringing a pet difficult, expensive, and inconvenient.

https://www.nps.gov/kova

Resources

Acadia National Park (U.S. National Park Service). (n.d.). https://w *ww.nps.gov/acad/index.htm*

Amphibians - Denali National Park & Preserve (U.S. National Park Service). (n.d.). https://www.nps.gov/dena/learn/nature/amphibi *ans.htm*

Arches National Park (U.S. National Park Service). (n.d.). https://w *ww.nps.gov/arch/index.htm*

B.A.R.K. Ranger Program (U.S. National Park Service). (n.d.). https://www.nps.gov/articles/000/be-a-hot-springs-bark-r anger.htm

Bark Ranger - New River Gorge National Park & Preserve (U.S. National Park Service). (n.d.). https://www.nps.gov/neri/planyour *visit/bark-ranger.htm*

BAT Flight Program - Carlsbad Caverns National Park (U.S. National Park Service). (n.d.). https://www.nps.gov/cave/planyourvisit/bat *_flight_program.htm*

Be a B.A.R.K. Ranger - PETs (U.S. National Park Service). (n.d.). https://www.nps.gov/subjects/pets/be-a-bark-ranger.htm

Be an Acadia Bark Ranger (U.S. National Park Service). (n.d.). https://www.nps.gov/articles/be-an-acadia-bark-ranger.ht m

Become a Biscayne B.A.R.K. Ranger (U.S. National Park Service). (n.d.). https://www.nps.gov/thingstodo/become-a-biscayne-b-a-r-k-ranger.htm

Big Bend National Park (U.S. National Park Service). (n.d.). *https://www.nps.gov/bibe/index.htm*

Biscayne National Park (U.S. National Park Service). (n.d.). *https://www.nps.gov/bisc/index.htm*

Black Canyon Of The Gunnison National Park (U.S. National Park Service). (n.d.). *https://www.nps.gov/blca/index.htm*

Bryce Canyon National Park (U.S. National Park Service). (n.d.). *https://www.nps.gov/brca/index.htm*

Camping with Pets - Camping (U.S. National Park Service). (n.d.). https://www.nps.gov/subjects/camping/camping-with-pets. htm

Canyonlands National Park (U.S. National Park Service). (n.d.). *https://www.nps.gov/cany/index.htm*

Capitol Reef National Park (U.S. National Park Service). (n.d.). *https://www.nps.gov/care/index.htm*

Carlsbad Caverns National Park (U.S. National Park Service). (n.d.).

https://www.nps.gov/cave/index.htm

Channel Islands National Park (U.S. National Park Service). (n.d.). *https://www.nps.gov/chis/index.htm*

Congaree National Park (U.S. National Park Service). (n.d.). *https://www.nps.gov/cong/index.htm*

Crater Lake National Park (U.S. National Park Service). (n.d.). *https://www.nps.gov/crla/index.htm*

Cuyahoga Valley National Park (U.S. National Park Service). (n.d.). *https://www.nps.gov/cuva/index.htm*

Death Valley National Park (U.S. National Park Service). (n.d.). *https://www.nps.gov/deva/index.htm*

Denali National Park & Preserve (U.S. National Park Service). (n.d.). *https://www.nps.gov/dena/index.htm*

Dry Tortugas National Park (U.S. National Park Service). (n.d.). *https://www.nps.gov/drto/index.htm*

Everglades National Park (U.S. National Park Service). (n.d.). *https://www.nps.gov/ever/index.htm*

Frequently asked questions – Katmai National Park & Preserve (U.S. National Park Service). (n.d.). *https://www.nps.gov/katm/faqs.ht m*

Gates Of The Arctic National Park & Preserve (U.S. National Park

Service). (n.d.). *https://www.nps.gov/gaar/index.htm*

Gateway Arch National Park (U.S. National Park Service). (n.d.). *https://www.nps.gov/jeff/index.htm*

Glacier Bay National Park & Preserve (U.S. National Park Service). (n.d.). *https://www.nps.gov/glba/index.htm*

Glacier National Park (U.S. National Park Service). (n.d.). *https://www.nps.gov/glac/index.htm*

Grand Canyon National Park (U.S. National Park Service). (n.d.). *https://www.nps.gov/grca/index.htm*

Grand Teton National Park (U.S. National Park Service). (n.d.). *https://www.nps.gov/grte/index.htm*

Great Basin National Park (U.S. National Park Service). (n.d.). *https://www.nps.gov/grba/index.htm*

Great Sand Dunes National Park & Preserve (U.S. National Park Service). (n.d.). *https://www.nps.gov/grsa/index.htm*

Great Smoky Mountains National Park (U.S. National Park Service). (n.d.). *https://www.nps.gov/grsm/index.htm*

Guadalupe Mountains National Park (U.S. National Park Service). (n.d.). *https://www.nps.gov/gumo/index.htm*

Haleakalā National Park (U.S. National Park Service). (n.d.). *https://www.nps.gov/hale/index.htm*

Hawaiʻi Volcanoes National Park (U.S. National Park Service). (n.d.). *https://www.nps.gov/havo/index.htm*

Hiking etiquette (U.S. National Park Service). (n.d.). https://www.nps.gov/articles/hikingetiquette.htm

Hiking with Pets – Trails & Hiking (U.S. National Park Service). (n.d.). https://www.nps.gov/subjects/trails/hiking-with-pets.htm

Hot Springs National Park (U.S. National Park Service). (n.d.). *https://www.nps.gov/hosp/index.htm*

I Didn't Know That!: Hiking with Pets (U.S. National Park Service). (n.d.). *https://www.nps.gov/articles/ooo/idkt_pets.htm*

Indiana Dunes National Park (U.S. National Park Service). (n.d.). *https://www.nps.gov/indu/index.htm*

INDU BARK Rangers – Indiana Dunes National Park (U.S. National Park Service). (n.d.). *https://www.nps.gov/indu/planyourvisit/bark-rangers.htm*

Isle Royale National Park (U.S. National Park Service). (n.d.). *https://www.nps.gov/isro/index.htm*

Joshua Trees – Joshua Tree National Park (U.S. National Park Service). (n.d.). *https://www.nps.gov/jotr/learn/nature/jtrees.htm*

Joshua Tree National Park (U.S. National Park Service). (n.d.). *https://www.nps.gov/jotr/index.htm*

Katmai National Park & Preserve (U.S. National Park Service). (n.d.). *https://www.nps.gov/katm/index.htm*

Kenai Fjords National Park (U.S. National Park Service). (n.d.). *https://www.nps.gov/kefj/index.htm*

Kobuk Valley National Park (U.S. National Park Service). (n.d.). *https://www.nps.gov/kova/index.htm*

Lake Clark National Park & Preserve (U.S. National Park Service). (n.d.). *https://www.nps.gov/lacl/index.htm*

Lassen Volcanic National Park (U.S. National Park Service). (n.d.). *https://www.nps.gov/lavo/index.htm*

Learn about the park – Big Bend National Park (U.S. National Park Service). (n.d.). *https://www.nps.gov/bibe/learn/index.htm*

Mammoth Cave National Park (U.S. National Park Service). (n.d.). *https://www.nps.gov/maca/index.htm*

Mesa Verde National Park (U.S. National Park Service). (n.d.). *https://www.nps.gov/meve/index.htm*

Mount Rainier National Park (U.S. National Park Service). (n.d.). *https://www.nps.gov/mora/index.htm*

National Park of American Samoa (U.S. National Park Service). (n.d.). *https://www.nps.gov/npsa/index.htm*

Natural Features & Ecosystems – Big Bend National Park (U.S.

*National Park Service). (n.d.). https://www.nps.gov/bibe/learn/
nature/naturalfeaturesandecosystems.htm*

*Nature – Katmai National Park & Preserve (U.S. National Park
Service). (n.d.). https://www.nps.gov/katm/learn/nature/index.
htm*

*New River Gorge National Park & Preserve (U.S. National Park
Service). (n.d.). https://www.nps.gov/neri/index.htm*

*North Cascades National Park (U.S. National Park Service). (n.d.).
https://www.nps.gov/noca/index.htm*

*Olympic National Park (U.S. National Park Service). (n.d.). https://w
ww.nps.gov/olym/index.htm*

*Petrified Forest National Park (U.S. National Park Service). (n.d.).
https://www.nps.gov/pefo/index.htm*

PETs – Arches National Park (U.S. National Park Service). (n.d.).
https://www.nps.gov/arch/planyourvisit/pets.htm

*PETs – Big Bend National Park (U.S. National Park Service). (n.d.).
https://www.nps.gov/bibe/planyourvisit/pets.htm*

*PETS – Biscayne National Park (U.S. National Park Service). (n.d.).
https://www.nps.gov/bisc/planyourvisit/pets.htm*

PETS – Bryce Canyon National Park (U.S. National Park Service).
(n.d.). *https://www.nps.gov/brca/planyourvisit/pets.htm*

PETS – Canyonlands National Park (U.S. National Park Service). (n.d.). *https://www.nps.gov/cany/planyourvisit/pets.htm*

PETS – Capitol Reef National Park (U.S. National Park Service). (n.d.). *https://www.nps.gov/care/planyourvisit/pets.htm*

PETS – Channel Islands National Park (U.S. National Park Service). (n.d.). *https://www.nps.gov/chis/planyourvisit/pets.htm*

PETs – Crater Lake National Park (U.S. National Park Service). (n.d.). *https://www.nps.gov/crla/planyourvisit/pets.htm*

PETS – Congaree National Park (U.S. National Park Service). (n.d.). *https://www.nps.gov/cong/planyourvisit/pets.htm*

Pets – Cuyahoga Valley National Park (U.S. National Park Service). (n.d.). *https://www.nps.gov/cuva/planyourvisit/pets.htm*

PETS – Death Valley National Park (U.S. National Park Service). (n.d.). *https://www.nps.gov/deva/planyourvisit/pets.htm*

PETS – Denali National Park & Preserve (U.S. National Park Service). (n.d.). *https://www.nps.gov/dena/planyourvisit/pets.htm*

PETs – Dry Tortugas National Park (U.S. National Park Service). (n.d.). *https://www.nps.gov/drto/planyourvisit/pets.htm*

PETS – Everglades National Park (U.S. National Park Service). (n.d.). *https://www.nps.gov/ever/planyourvisit/pets.htm*

Pets – Gates Of The Arctic National Park & Preserve (U.S. National

Park Service). (n.d.). https://www.nps.gov/gaar/planyourvisit/pet s.htm

PETS – Gateway Arch National Park (U.S. National Park Service). (n.d.). *https://www.nps.gov/jeff/planyourvisit/pets.htm*

PETS – Glacier Bay National Park & Preserve (U.S. National Park Service). (n.d.). *https://www.nps.gov/glba/planyourvisit/pets.htm*

PETS – Glacier National Park (U.S. National Park Service). (n.d.). https://www.nps.gov/glac/planyourvisit/pets.htm

PETS – Grand Canyon National Park (U.S. National Park Service). (n.d.). *https://www.nps.gov/grca/planyourvisit/pets.htm*

PETS – Grand Teton National Park (U.S. National Park Service). (n.d.). *https://www.nps.gov/grte/planyourvisit/pets.htm*

PETs – Great Basin National Park (U.S. National Park Service). (n.d.). *https://www.nps.gov/grba/planyourvisit/pets.htm*

PETs – Great Sand Dunes National Park & Preserve (U.S. National Park Service). (n.d.). *https://www.nps.gov/grsa/planyourvisit/pets .htm*

PEts – Great Smoky Mountains National Park (U.S. National Park Service). (n.d.). *https://www.nps.gov/grsm/planyourvisit/pets.ht m*

PETs – Guadalupe Mountains National Park (U.S. National Park Service). (n.d.). *https://www.nps.gov/gumo/planyourvisit/pets.ht*

m

PETS - Haleakalā National Park (U.S. National Park Service). (n.d.). *https://www.nps.gov/hale/planyourvisit/pets.htm*

PETS - Hawai'i Volcanoes National Park (U.S. National Park Service). (n.d.). *https://www.nps.gov/havo/planyourvisit/pets.htm*

PETs - Hot Springs National Park (U.S. National Park Service). (n.d.). *https://www.nps.gov/hosp/planyourvisit/pets.htm*

PETS - Indiana Dunes National Park (U.S. National Park Service). (n.d.). *https://www.nps.gov/indu/planyourvisit/pets.htm*

PETS - Isle Royale National Park (U.S. National Park Service). (n.d.). *https://www.nps.gov/isro/planyourvisit/pets.htm*

Pets - Joshua Tree National Park (U.S. National Park Service). (n.d.). *https://www.nps.gov/jotr/planyourvisit/pets.htm*

PETS - Kenai Fjords National Park (U.S. National Park Service). (n.d.). *https://www.nps.gov/kefj/planyourvisit/pets.htm*

PETS - Lake Clark National Park & Preserve (U.S. National Park Service). (n.d.). *https://www.nps.gov/lacl/planyourvisit/pets.htm*

PETs - Lassen Volcanic National Park (U.S. National Park Service). (n.d.). *https://www.nps.gov/lavo/planyourvisit/pets.htm*

PETs - Mammoth Cave National Park (U.S. National Park Service). (n.d.). *https://www.nps.gov/maca/planyourvisit/pets.htm*

PETs – Mesa Verde National Park (U.S. National Park Service). (n.d.). *https://www.nps.gov/meve/planyourvisit/pets.htm*

PETs – Mount Rainier National Park (U.S. National Park Service). (n.d.). *https://www.nps.gov/mora/planyourvisit/pets.htm*

PETS – National Park of American Samoa (U.S. National Park Service). (n.d.). *https://www.nps.gov/npsa/planyourvisit/pets.htm*

PETS – New River Gorge National Park & Preserve (U.S. National Park Service). (n.d.). *https://www.nps.gov/neri/planyourvisit/pets. htm*

PETs – North Cascades National Park (U.S. National Park Service). (n.d.). *https://www.nps.gov/noca/planyourvisit/pets.htm*

PETS – Olympic National Park (U.S. National Park Service). (n.d.). https://www.nps.gov/olym/planyourvisit/pets.htm

PETS – Petrified Forest National Park (U.S. National Park Service). (n.d.). *https://www.nps.gov/pefo/planyourvisit/pets.htm*

PETs – Pinnacles National Park (U.S. National Park Service). (n.d.). *https://www.nps.gov/pinn/planyourvisit/pets.htm*

Pets. Please follow the rules of BARK! – Redwood National and State Parks (U.S. National Park Service). (n.d.). *https://www.nps.gov/ redw/planyourvisit/pets.htm*

PETS – Rocky Mountain National Park (U.S. National Park Service). (n.d.). *https://www.nps.gov/romo/planyourvisit/pets.htm*

PETS – Saguaro National Park (U.S. National Park Service). (n.d.). https://www.nps.gov/sagu/planyourvisit/pets.htm

PETs – Sequoia & Kings Canyon National Parks (U.S. National Park Service). (n.d.). *https://www.nps.gov/seki/planyourvisit/pets.htm*

Pets – Shenandoah National Park (U.S. National Park Service). (n.d.). *https://www.nps.gov/shen/planyourvisit/pets.htm*

PETS – Theodore Roosevelt National Park (U.S. National Park Service). (n.d.). *https://www.nps.gov/thro/planyourvisit/pets.htm*

PETS (U.S. National Park Service). (n.d.). https://www.nps.gov/subjects/pets/index.htm

PETS – Virgin Islands National Park (U.S. National Park Service). (n.d.). *https://www.nps.gov/viis/planyourvisit/pets.htm*

PETs – Voyageurs National Park (U.S. National Park Service). (n.d.). *https://www.nps.gov/voya/planyourvisit/pets.htm*

PETS – Wind Cave National Park (U.S. National Park Service). (n.d.). *https://www.nps.gov/wica/planyourvisit/pets.htm*

PETS – White Sands National Park (U.S. National Park Service). (n.d.). *https://www.nps.gov/whsa/planyourvisit/pets.htm*

Pets – Wrangell – St Elias National Park & Preserve (U.S. National Park Service). (n.d.). *https://www.nps.gov/wrst/planyourvisit/pets.htm*

PETs – Yellowstone National Park (U.S. National Park Service). (n.d.). *https://www.nps.gov/yell/planyourvisit/pets.htm*

PETS – Yosemite National Park (U.S. National Park Service). (n.d.). *https://www.nps.gov/yose/planyourvisit/pets.htm*

PETS – Zion National Park (U.S. National Park Service). (n.d.). https://www.nps.gov/zion/planyourvisit/pets.htm

Pets at Black Canyon – Black Canyon Of The Gunnison National Park (U.S. National Park Service). (n.d.). *https://www.nps.gov/ blca/planyourvisit/pets2.htm*

Pinnacles National Park (U.S. National Park Service). (n.d.). *https://www.nps.gov/pinn/index.htm*

Redwood National and State Parks (U.S. National Park Service). (n.d.). *https://www.nps.gov/redw/index.htm*

Rocky Mountain National Park (U.S. National Park Service). (n.d.). *https://www.nps.gov/romo/index.htm*

Saguaro National Park (U.S. National Park Service). (n.d.). *https://w ww.nps.gov/sagu/index.htm*

Sequoia & Kings Canyon National Parks (U.S. National Park Service). (n.d.). *https://www.nps.gov/seki/index.htm*

Service Animals – Accessibility (U.S. National Park Service). (n.d.). https://www.nps.gov/subjects/accessibility/service-animals. htm

Shenandoah National Park (U.S. National Park Service). (n.d.). *https://www.nps.gov/shen/index.htm*

Ten Essentials (U.S. National Park Service). (n.d.). https://www.nps.gov/articles/10essentials.htm

The 11 Essentials for hiking in the Guadalupe Mountains (U.S. National Park Service). (n.d.). *https://www.nps.gov/articles/000/gumo_11essentials.htm*

Theodore Roosevelt National Park (U.S. National Park Service). (n.d.). *https://www.nps.gov/thro/index.htm*

Traveling with Pets – Carlsbad Caverns National Park (U.S. National Park Service). (n.d.). *https://www.nps.gov/cave/planyourvisit/pets.htm*

Virgin Islands National Park (U.S. National Park Service). (n.d.). *https://www.nps.gov/viis/index.htm*

Visiting with pets – Acadia National Park (U.S. National Park Service). (n.d.). *https://www.nps.gov/acad/planyourvisit/pets.htm*

Voyageurs National Park (U.S. National Park Service). (n.d.). *https://www.nps.gov/voya/index.htm*

White Sands National Park (U.S. National Park Service). (n.d.). *https://www.nps.gov/whsa/index.htm*

Wildlife – Denali National Park & Preserve (U.S. National Park Service). (n.d.). *https://www.nps.gov/dena/learn/nature/wildlif*

e.htm

Wind Cave National Park (U.S. National Park Service). (n.d.). *https://www.nps.gov/wica/index.htm*

Wrangell – St Elias National Park & Preserve (U.S. National Park Service). (n.d.). *https://www.nps.gov/wrst/index.htm*

Yellowstone National Park (U.S. National Park Service). (n.d.). *https://www.nps.gov/yell/index.htm*

Yosemite National Park (U.S. National Park Service). (n.d.). *https://www.nps.gov/yose/index.htm*

Zion National Park (U.S. National Park Service). (n.d.). https://www.nps.gov/zion/index.htm

www.ingramcontent.com/pod-product-compliance
Lightning Source LLC
Chambersburg PA
CBHW060253150626
46553CB00019BA/2217